MENTAL MODELS

Enhanced Ability to Reason and Make Decisions

(Develop Mental Models and Learn Problem
Solving to Take Better Decisions)

James Segrest

Published By James Segrest

James Segrest

Mental Models: Enhanced Ability to Reason and Make Decisions (Develop Mental Models and Learn Problem Solving to Take Better Decisions)

ISBN 978-1-77485-398-6

TABLE OF CONTENTS

Introduction

This book provides essential information on how you can effectively utilize different mental models to improve the quality of your thoughts behavior, attitudes, and thoughts. Mental models form the basis for how you see and comprehend the realities of the world. Beyond your thinking, they reflect on the way you interact with others around you. Therefore having the correct mental models can help you to be seen as a highly competent and well-liked person.

In its simplest terms mental modelling is the idea of simplifying information to convert this information into useful points. If you were able to master this, you'd be able react more effectively and faster , without sacrificing the quality of your thinking and choices.

When taken at a high level, helpful mental models could become potentially damaging schemas, including stereotypes, prejudices, and different kinds that are cognitive biases.

If you're currently struggling with inadequate conceptual models of your mind, you can be able to improve them with consistent practice and commitment. You can find out how to achieve this as well as more, by studying and analyzing the content in this text.

Thank you to you for downloading the book. I hope you enjoy it!

Chapter 1: Is A History Of Popular Mental Models

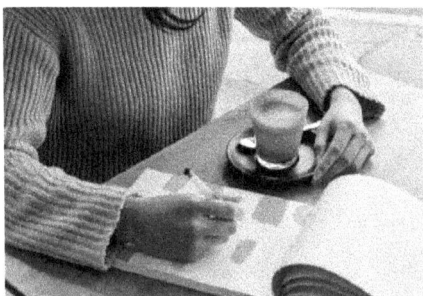

Elon Musk and the First Principles Mental Model

If you've used the internet during the last couple of years, you'll know whom Elon Musk. He is the chief executive officer of Tesla, a car maker that focuses on mass production of affordable electric vehicles solar roofs, solar cars, and battery-powered products. He's the brains responsible for PayPal which was founded as X.com and later was acquired through eBay (making Musk his first billion dollar company).

When he was ten years old at the time, he learned how to program computers. Then, when he was twelve the first time he sold his creation (a video game known as Blastar). Musk is currently involved in some groundbreaking projects, like Nueralink which is a tiny device inside the brain that can connect via Bluetooth to smartphones. Simply put, Elon Musk might be one of the most innovative and successful people in the world today using mental models to help him achieve his goals.

One particular model that Musk is well-known for his use of in interviews is referred to as"the first principle model. The model goes all the way into the Classical period (and even to the Greek philosopher who probably controlled you in your Psychology and English classes: Aristotle). Aristotle believed that each thought that was a new philosophical idea began by tracing the idea backwards until the philosopher arrived at the base beliefs that the belief was based on. Rene Descartes thought similarly that philosophy could be developed by questioning every aspect of the idea until he finally came to the basic truth hidden beneath the philosophy (one which could not be disbelieved since it was completely true). By using First Principles the famous philosophers sought to develop original ideas instead of examining other ideas and altering their ideas incrementally to create an entirely new version of the same idea. In simple terms the mental model aims to dissect complex problems to create original solutions.

The principle is based on looking at the complexity of the problem and it is, just like Aristotle and Descartes by reducing it to basic truths until it's broken down to the point that it is unable to be further deduced. When you apply the first principles approach it is not based on an analogy or the things you've seen instead, you will be able to draw conclusions by looking at the core of the issue. Instead of asking "How do I know this has been done before and how could I adapt that to my advantage," ask yourself, "What can I be certain is true in this case and how do I construct from that?".

The year 2002 was when Elon Musk decided to launch a rocket to Mars and it was never done before. Elon Musk embarked on a quest to accomplish this goal, but quickly hit a massive obstacle: rockets are costly. After looking all over the world with various aerospace firms, Musk discovered that a rocket could cost around $65 million. Famously, using the first principle conceptual model Musk was able to break down the issue (rockets are costly) by asking "What is the material that rockets are made of?" After compiling an ingredients list, he studied every product to determine their price as an individual item.

It turned out that purchasing the components needed to build a rocket was less than 2% of the cost of purchasing an already-built rocket. In this instance, applying the first principles model resulted in Musk making a rocket for himself, purchasing each component independently and then launching a revolutionary company for this: SpaceX.

Space Exploration Technologies Corporation was established in 2002, and is Musk's 3rd company. Since its inception, SpaceX has accomplished incredible things and has made history on a number of fronts. The year 2008 was the first time NASA gave SpaceX a deal to transport items for SpaceX's International Space Station for astronauts stationed there instead the company's shuttles. Elon Musk is a genius and his achievements can be attributed, at least in part, completely, due to his refusal to accept the status quo, and instead, he used an idea of mental models for thinking in a new method.

It's an amazing story, but we're all in the process of building rockets to launch into the outer space. There aren't many of us who are scientists, engineers or billionaires. However, we all face complex problems that are able to be reduced into solutions that are original. One of those difficult problems that we all face at some point in life is ever-present P-word: purpose.

It's one of those big life-long questions one must be able to answer in order to be completely satisfied. "What is my goal? What is my reason for being here? How can I be a positive influence?" Like anything else it is possible to follow a standard path to "finding your goal."

It usually starts with the time of high school graduation. As teens we try to condense our interests and abilities into one or a few words that can be incorporated into a college degree. We go to college and then graduate, we find a job and we start an entire family, and then we declare it over. If you've been kicked out of school, or if your journey didn't go like the one in that sentence suggested, you could be attempting to figure out the answers to that question. As a typical human you might be taking a look at what others do. You look through the list of skills for careers until you come across one that has you thinking, "Hey, I could accomplish this!" Then you boil it down to a major in college, attend school and complete your studies and wash, rinse, and repeat.

This is the typical way to answer the issue: "What is my purpose?" This is the way to buy an entire rocket, regardless of the fact that it's extremely expensive. What's an alternative?

It is possible to apply the same first-principles approach that brought Elon Musk success and fame. All you need to do is to simplify the things you'd like to accomplish by transforming your life into the smallestand most easily understood facts. If someone had told you in the beginning that you should become a special needs educator because you possess a special feeling of compassion for people with disabilities. The first principle mental model asks, "What do you know to be real?" In this case the only thing you can be sure of that is true that you have a comfortable relationship with people who have disabilities and feel a special sense of compassion for them.

It's true and you're able to accomplish anything using it, without having to conform to the same model that all others follow. You can develop products that improve the quality of life for those who are confined to wheelchairs. You could lead classes online or in person to teach people with disabilities how to treat people who have special needs with respect.

When you've reduced your passions and drive you to the simplest of shapes, you are able to dream to the extent you wish. It's not necessary to follow the path of someone else and make it your own life. You can create your own way and create your own lifestyle by starting from scratch and then emerge with a flourish, just as Elon Musk has done with SpaceX. This is the first-principles model.

Ivan Pavlov and Classical Conditioning

If you're interested in Psychology or had to complete an education course in general at one time, the name Ivan Pavlov could ring a bell. Pavlov was an Russian scientist who came across a chance discovery that transformed the world of psychological models and mental models for the better. The study he conducted wasn't focused on people but rather on animals: Pavlov was studying canines when this epiphany occurred.

It was the year 1890 and Pavlov's lab was occupied with dogs, and food for dog. He believed that when a bowl of food is served before the dog, it will trigger a reaction: salivating. His assistant would place a bowl of food before the dog, and then count the amount of saliva that the dog's mouth produced. As time passed but Pavlov noticed something was happening that he hadn't anticipated.

He observed that the dogs started to gag before they noticed the food being served to them. They began salivating when they heard Pavlov's assistant walk through the hallway to carry the food to the dining room. The dogs were able to learn that the steps of the assistant connected to the time of their meal and triggered the reaction that was salivating.

Incredulous, Pavlov began another series of experiments. He used an electronic metronome (similar to the beat of his assistant's feet tapping) in the presence of dogs. It's not surprising that just hearing the metronome did not make dogs want to eat. Then , he began to teach them called conditioning. It was when he played his metronome before feeding the dogs.

After repeating this process for a few times He played the metronome by itself without feeding the dogs anything to eat. However, at this point the dogs were aware that the sound of the metronome believed to be related to eating time. Even without receiving food, but this time, upon hearing the metronome's sounds the dogs started to squeak like their food was right before them.

Thirty years after a psychologist named John Watson reads about Pavlov's discoveries and asks his self, "Could classical conditioning work on humans too?" He decided to carry out a terrifying set of tests on a baby named Little Albert using the same method of experimentation Pavlov had employed on his dogs. Watson gave the baby nine months old a number of objects and recorded his reactions to them (much as

Pavlov playing the metronome in the beginning of the test).

Little Albert was quite calm when confronted by rabbits, a white rat and even masks that were scary. What Watson did discover, however the fact how making a noisy sound behind Little Albert's head scared the child so much that he'd cry out instantly (in this instance, Albert crying out of fear is linked to dogs that are salivating because of desire). Watson was then able to begin conditioning the infant.

He would display to Little Albert the white rat and, soon after, he'd make the loud sound right to the left of Little Albert to scare him (the equivalent to Pavlov playing the metronome, and then showing the food item). After seven attempts across seven months, Little Albert just had to be able to see the white rat once before his tears would erupt and scream without the terrifying sound never occurring.

Albert had discovered that the rodent was associated with a frightening, loud sound.

Like the dogs learned through connection that the metronome signified food was on the way, Albert learned that the rodent meant that a frightening sound was about to come.

This was only the beginning. Classical conditioning goes far beyond than simply salivating dogs or frightening babies. It is true that, regardless of whether you realize it or not classical conditioning is already present in your life. Do you remember the time when you contracted food poisoning following a cookout and then decided not to consume hot dogs? What about the time you had a drink too much tequila and staring into the glass the following day made you feel sick? All of these are an illustration of the classical conditioning. Your body is accustomed to combining smoking hot dogs and tequila to throwing up.

However, if the event was only once instead of a series of trials throughout time, your relationship is less strong. You could find yourself eating hot dogs and drinking tequila within a matter of minutes. Imagine putting this mental model in practice in order to accomplish goals that aren't enjoyable to accomplish by themselves.

For instance, every time you get up to plan your budget you treat yourself to an latte or a chocolate bar. After a few trials over a number of weeks, thinking about your electric bill or car loan might cause you to smile when you think of foamed milk, or melting chocolate. If you are able to connect something routine such as completing your budget with something that is enjoyable such as a latte you might be looking forward to checking on how your bank account is doing. Training yourself in this manner means you'll find a way to incorporate bad behaviors that need to be implemented into your daily routine often. Let's go through the stages of classical conditioning, and then see how to do it.

There are a few crucial terms to understand before beginning your own classic conditioning exercise.

* A stimulus that is unconditioned triggers an inherently unconditioned stimulus.

* A neutral stimulus creates no response.

* The combination of the non-conditioned stimulus and neutral stimulus triggers an conditioned response since the stimulus that is unconditioned is present.

It's a lot complex than it actually is. It's possible you can, I'm sure. Keep going! The first two connected terms are the 'unconditioned stimuli, which triggers an unconditioned response. In Pavlov's test the stimulus that was unconditioned was food, and the unconditioned reaction to the stimuli was salivating. For Little Albert his unconditioned stimulus was a scary sound and his unconditioned response to the scary sound was crying.

In simple terms the definition of an unconditioned stimulus is an event that occurs in your everyday life that triggers the response you desire without any instruction or training required. If an unconditioned stimulus is presented to you, it is likely that you will naturally respond to it. If you're already fond of chocolate (unconditioned stimulus) the response you get when you consume this (joy!) does not require any learning. Chocolate eating (unconditioned stimulus) brings happiness (unconditioned reaction). If you are looking for a reason to do this, pick an unconditioned stimulus or reward, that stimulates you to do something accomplished in order to be able to enjoy it! Are you still with me?

The second word can be described as "neutral stimuli." To Pavlov it was the sound of the metronome. For Little Albert the stimulus was watching the white rat by itself. For us this is the taxing or irritating thing that you ought to do but don't want perform. Perhaps it's budgeting. Budgeting, or any other annoying habit you'd like to train you to accept (neutral stimuli) is, as of now, produces no reaction from you.

This is the most difficult part. When the chocolate (unconditioned stimulus) triggers the emotion of joy (unconditioned response) When it's coupled by the budgeting (neutral stimulus) that usually does not trigger any responses, then the combination of these two (unconditioned stimuli and neutral) can trigger joy, the stimulus that is now conditioned. Do you see what's happening? Your mind is being trained to believe that budgeting can be as enjoyable as chocolate. Let's look at this one more:

Unconditioned stimuli trigger the unconditioned reaction.

o Chocolate elicits joy.

* A neutral stimulus creates no response.

A Budgeting exercise does not trigger any reaction.

* The combination of the non-conditioned stimulus and neutral stimulus causes an conditioned response since the stimulus unconditioned is present.

A chocolate snack while on a budget brings joy since chocolate is in the menu.

You are now attempting. What is an unpleasant habit or task you should be doing more frequently? What is a motivating motive force that you can be rewarded with to accomplish the task? Perhaps you'd like less soda, and then replace it with having more water. It's possible to keep a soda and water bottle on you throughout the day. Each when you've finished the water bottle, you'll get to consume a soda.

Perhaps you're having a hard getting up early in the morning, and this makes you late for work (who hasn't experienced this?). You can buy a specific type or espresso (or the coffee creamer) and give yourself a treat when you wake up and get out of bed and don't hit the snooze button again. Whatever it is you do classical conditioning is an ideal mental model that will definitely aid.

Tips to make use of Pavlov's Classical Conditioning:

* Don't get caught over the language. Pick a thing you're not a fan of but wish you could do more often. Pair it with something you enjoy doing. It's as easy as that.

* The trick to use such a mental model is to practice it over time. Remember that little Albert was not afraid of the white rodent when the experiment began. Seven weeks later, and after seven distinct trails, that the conditioning began to take hold. You should allow yourself at least a month before you make the decision to quit.

* Select an unconditioned stimuli (or reward) that's easily accessible (and preferably that it doesn't require someone else to carry out). The goal is for your unconditioned reward to be available to

ensure that you don't have to spend a day without your chocolate.

Charlie Munger, Warren Buffet and Cognitive Biases

Dairy Queen and Pampered Chef If you've not seen these two giants in the history of mental models, chances are you've seen these two companies that they own through their business. Berkshire Hathaway is the fourth-largest publicly traded company in the world and its Vice Chairman and CEO use an array of more than one hundred mental models in order to take financial decisions.

Warren Buffet and Charlie Munger are two men who hail from Omaha, Nebraska. They became acquainted through an acquaintance at a dinner party in Omaha when they discovered that they worked in the same local supermarket as teens. The the rest is history. The pair has been friends for more than sixty years and have been business partners for more than four decades.

Warren Buffet has had a aptitude for finance since childhood, purchasing his first stock when he was eleven and establishing various businesses when he was an teen, including an incredibly profitable business for pinball machines in the local barbershops. He earned his degree in the class of Columbia University and began work in an law company located in New York with his mentor.

When the firm dissolved, Buffet returned home to establish his own company, Buffet Partnerships, in 1956. The business rapidly grew in fortune after it expanded into seven partnerships and by the age of 32, Buffet enjoyed life as millionaire. Then, Buffet merged the partnerships (first as a textiles business and later a move to insurance) which is when Berkshire Hathaway was born.

In the meantime, Charlie Munger attended Harvard Law School and was a co-founder of the law firm Munger, Tolles, & Olson, LLP (which still exists to this day). Buffet eventually persuaded Munger to quit the firm to realize his full potential as vice chairman of Berkshire Hathaway in 1978. The two of them, who have a an estimated net worth of more than $80 billion continue to work without news of retirement announcement at some point in the future, even when they are 95 and 88 years old.

Their wealth and achievements are, yes in part, due to their commitment in their mental model. What's unique and distinctive with this particular partnership, in comparison those two model we've examined to date is the fact that Munger and Buffet do not choose a single mental model for their choices: They choose to use a variety of mental models.

Chapter 2: Thinking As A Modulation

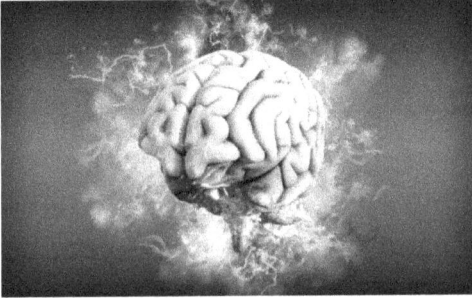

"... in truth, there was no and will never be any one who will know regarding the gods and the things I'm talking about. The only thing that matters is opinion. most important thing." This was the quote from French philosopher Michel de Montaigne.

From the evolutionary viewpoint From an evolutionary perspective, the main difference between animated and inanimate nature, as per his view is that it is "a prominent reflection of reality." The ability to respond quickly and effectively to changes in the environment is essential to the survival of living organisms over the process of evolution.

L.S. Vygotsky: "We see only one tiny portion of the universe Our feelings provide us peace through excerpts, or the smallest of details that matter to us. The psyche is the organ that allows for selection, or the sievethat filters the world, and changing it in order to take action. This is the positive function of the psyche not in reflection (it is a mirror of the mental one while The thermometer has more precision than sensation) However, it's not always reflecting correctly, i.e. the perception of reality is distorted to favor your organism. "

It is fundamentally sensitive. It is not able to provide organisms with an entire picture of reality. Only that is essential to the existence of the species within their ecological niche. It is always a matter of selective observation. It is essential to select an object, a particular job, that has an interest, perspective, issue or other.

It is crucial for the body to comprehend the issue, explain it, and interpret it according to the knowledge it has. Without this interpretation, it "does do not understand" what plan of action it should follow. Unidentified circumstances, an unsolved problem, suggests an imminent danger for the body.

If I am aware of a particular circumstance, I create an image of the situation using the blocks of my model of the world, i.e. I project my image of reality onto scene. I project my knowledge from the past onto the present situation, and then accept the imposed knowledge as truth.

"We don't define the world we experience. We only see what we are able to describe." -- Rene Descartes. This projection, or a part of my concept of the world, that "responded" with external stimuli as real!

Transformation of the image and the context

If the issue is solved as well as the picture is incorporated and incorporated into the image of our world it signifies that the image that we see of our world is changing. Now it is enriched by the knowledge gained from solving the issue. If you've successfully completed the task and the exercise has demonstrated the validity of your solution, when you have another encounter with an issue, you won't be able to solve it. Moreover you won't see the issue as a challenge and you'll be able to recognize the problem and implement the already-designed solution. Thinking about solving problems, or thinking through them, is often regarded as modeling, as a "game" using an image of reality that is created in our mind's space.

"Our opinions are based on our prejudices which have been formed since we were the age of 18." -- A. Einstein.

Comparative characteristics of mental models from the social and physical world

Mental models that are based on physical world objects. mental models of objects of society and human-machine systems

The spatial relationships between elements of the object are represented in the mind's space. These spatial relations can be transferred to an external plan by way of diagrams, drawings and further drawings. The attitudes of people towards one another within the family, the work environment, the attitude of workers towards society, and the attitudes of an individual toward a machine -- all of these relationships cannot be observed from outside and are able to change. It's not obvious that the situation in question is it appropriate to reflect them in the mind of an observer from the outside. (Exception of "staged" instances in the theater, literature, and the visual arts).

The processes that aren't perceived by the senses, are recorded in the mind's space via measurement instruments' readings (speedometers manometers, voltmeters and so on.) There aren't any comparable measuring instruments. Instruments that are of that "lie detector" kind are not considered to be measuring as they measure the physiological responses of the body by the measurement of only physical variables - pressure pulse and electrical resistance of skin, and so on.

To create models, a highly developed mathematical apparatus theories and calculation models for the applied disciplines of (materials electrical engineering etc.) are utilized. Formal models are constructed. is a challenge. In the field of psychology, the application of mathematicians does not go beyond the principles of Weber-Fechner as well as Stevens (opened at the beginning of the century) as well as statistical methods for data processing as well as mathematical models of certain psychophysiological functions

Verbal descriptions are applied with a fairly specific vocabulary. The language spoken in everyday use has more interpretability and, consequently, less precision.

The test for utility, instrumentality, and conformity of the real world is practice: the mental models that have been verified and proven to be useful in practice are kept and defended. The value of practice as a test of the value of the mental model is restricted by the following circumstances. Because the social system is a living thing with an internal memory as well as its own actions every experiment will be absorbed by the system and it is transformed into a new system.

The primary limitation in the human mind's knowledge

Another fundamental aspect that is the main difference between psychological models that describe the physical from the social realms. The central element in any social system is the human. Knowing how the system functions is achievable only with the help of the human. The only instrument we have to gain knowledge is our verbal, logical and thought. It is thought that is situated within the realm of consciousness and which produces products consist of text or formulas, as well as drawings. Drawings can be passed between people. However, we discovered that the biggest function in our lives is that of the unconscious portion in the brain. Is it possible for conscious (part in the psyche) be aware of the entire of the psyche? Does a small part of the psyche comprehend the entire psyche? The answer is clear and is no.

Human thought is, to put it simply isn't well-adapted to modeling the social environment.

Reality and thought models

Then you will be able to answer the question regarding the relation between mental models and real life. Mental models are tools for orienting us to the world outside and for solving problems. The sole criterion that determines the effectiveness of the model is its predictive power -- its capability to anticipate the behaviour of real objects. When we refer to our model as "correct", "okay", "true", we just replace the following notion by one word within its two possible meanings: "I believe in this model as I have performed actions based on it in these circumstances, and the outcomes of my actions were satisfactory to my "and" I am convinced of this model because I trust people who are convinced of the validity of it. If we choose to use "Actually ..." or "Actually the world is as it appears ..." the world is like this" we are fundamentally wrong. We can, at best, use a few models that have proven themselves in the past under concrete circumstances,

The "physical" strategies are confirmed by the subsequent actions that follow in the world of physical reality. These actions are extremely reliable and uncompromising judges of our decisions. If the pedestrian is mistaken in his prediction regarding the velocity of an approaching vehicle, he'll die as will his prediction. However, it's a different matter if the reflection of reality is part of a social system. When we encounter a difficult situation that involves human involvement. This particular situation, just like others, triggers anxiety, and a negative emotional backdrop and calls for solutions by "matching" the picture of the situation to a mental model that corresponds to the image. What's the solution?

In the vast majority of instances our "social" decisions don't impact our survival in the physical world. The mechanism for their verification practice is not present. The freedom to make decisions arbitrary is not restricted.

The second reason is that human solutions to problems in the world of social interaction are merely interpretations, and do not contribute to forecasting the behaviour that social structures. In the absence of accountability for arbitrary interpretations, this is the primary feature in mental representations of the world of social.

In the third place, because of the inability to recognize the social system as well as the absence of any practice as a standard for "truth" An arbitrary connection (concatenation or a match) of the picture of the current situation with the model of the subject's life is the answer to the issue. The coherence of the image to the current system of knowledge and concepts is interpreted as trust in the correctness of one's own understanding as a feeling of knowing the world (although it's in reality the projection of subjective thoughts to the universe) it is a feeling of inner peace and tranquility. Because in reflecting on social reality quality, accuracy, and the accuracy of reflection are not possible and the purpose of tackling problems is to feel positive emotions that are founded on self-confidence as well as the certainty of your own mind, regardless of what you think of yourself as reflecting the world. Absurdity is an assertion or belief that is opposite to what we consider to be true.

A sloppy and uncritical approach to their perception of reality can lead to bad, ineffective choices and, in the end, the inefficiency of businesses. Alternatives for "illusory" thinking arrogance, arrogance, and confidence can be an intelligent culture which is reflected by recognizing the world's complexity and the limits of our cognitive capabilities.

Fourthly, the unintentional interpretation of external events which doesn't result in any consequences or actions is the mainstay of our daily mental activities. Human brains are remarkably versatile and can easily produce a variety of theories of events. If one interpretation proves to be false then it can be quickly and easily replaced with another one that is similarly arbitrary. Humans have a remarkable flexibility. thinking is the most significant evolutionary achievement, which allows the individual to remain self-confident and discover solutions under the circumstances of time and information deficit. But, the flexibility of our thinking, which is a rational choice as well as in the social realm, frequently leads to poor quality choices. In reality, the purpose in this text is to comprehend what limitations we have to our thinking , and to find ways to overcome its weaknesses.

In the dynamics of groups and in communicative behaviour, a large space is taken up by the conflict of differing interpretations of similar events or facts regarding them.

Fifth, an accurateand and unambiguous prediction of the actions that social networks exhibit is not possible. Their predictions are always probabilistic.

Chapter 3: The Major Mental Models

Mental models aren't only influencing our thoughts, but they also influence our behavior. Every all the time, even when we're conscious of it. With only a few mental models in our arsenal it is inevitable that we establish patterns of behavior that are familiar to us as our thinking and decision-making are limited by the mental models we've got. If difficulties arise, we naturally fall back to familiar patterns to overcome them or just accept the fact that we will have to deal with the challenges.

If you are unable to think differently or modify your mindset It becomes hard to identify new possibilities or overcome current obstacles. We live in a world that is populated by elements of physics, biology psychology, psychology, and numerous other fields. We live in a multidisciplinary world where diverse elements interact in a healthy ecosystem. It is crucial to be aware of the major ideas or models across the various disciplines.

For example, if we take a look at the principle of reciprocity within the field of physics, which states that for each action there exists an equally opposing reaction. It might have its origins in physics but it also cuts across all aspects of our lives. Understanding that for each choice you make, there is consequences that force you to think about the consequences of your choices with the end result in mind, in the end, making your choices better thought-out.

Models like reciprocity show that in the body of knowledge, there are essential concepts and mental models must be part of our arsenal if we want to gain a complete knowledge of our world, and the way it operates. The choice of a specific field of expertise limit your possibilities, options and capacity to be able to change with an constantly changing world.

If you build a wide range of mental models each model is built upon each other and is interlinked based on the same concepts. The links form a network of mental models that create an effective system for thinking in filtering and analyzing information. The process of developing mental models is the process of integrating of knowledge acquired and experience. This integration allows inferences to be drawn from previous experiences.

Experience is an essential component to the construction of models for mental processing. Mental models are crucial to understand scenarios and systems. Through the creation of simple mental representations for complex systems, and events mental models improve our understanding of the various phenomena and how they function.

Mental models affect the way we think;

* Organising information and knowledge in a manner that we comprehend it.

* Making references from experiences from the past.

* Linking concepts related to produce procedural knowledge.

Mental models help us to anticipate the possible outcomes of various scenarios using mental simulations.

Each mental model is an individual perspective and outlook on life. An array of diverse models will increase your capacity to solve problems, ideas generation, and making decisions. If we have an extensive mental model latticework that we can expand our options to deal with various situations, and also our capacity to alter our behavior and actions according to the circumstance in front of us. If you have more models of your mind that you can use, the more the range of thoughts and, consequently, the greater the possibilities you will be able to recognize.

Mental models are continually created and refined during regular thinking. They are created through the organization of knowledge and details, as well as simulations of processes and previous experiences. Mental models help the process of identifying potential opportunities, resolving problems , and developing ideas to meet our requirements. Innovations in fields like technology, medicine and engineering are based on the ability to innovate determined by the imagination of the ideas we can generate.

The major fields and disciplines, like biology, physics or economics, depend on the fundamental mental models used to help in the learning process and further progress through the development of innovative and problem-solving capabilities. Frameworks for mental models that integrate the knowledge of diverse fields to create multiple-disciplinary representations of mental models that are utilized widely to clarify situations across diverse disciplines and bodies of information. Interconnected models that link concepts from various fields form an interconnected model with the ability to be used in a wide range of situations and systems.

The Mental Models of Psychology

Mental models affect our thinking and decision-making process. We draw our conclusions based upon our beliefs or prejudices, feelings and experience. That means that our perceptions are influenced by our individual beliefs. Our beliefs affect our perceptions by causing us to view things in a manner which confirms the assumptions we already hold. In this situation it becomes very difficult to alter our thinking and behavior patterns due to the fact that we have rigid or fixed expectations that guide us to determine and evaluate the world, people, and systems.

A Ladder to Inference

The human mind takes up less than two seconds. Therefore, it's hard to recognize our automatic reactions since they happen instinctively. Each of us gives significance to our observations and then base our decisions on the meanings that we've come up with. The ladder of inference constructed by Senge is a seven-step method of reasoning and thinking.

We choose facts from our own experiences and various occasions. These observations and facts, depending on the meanings we assign them are the basis for the assumptions we form about the incident. Based on these assumptions, draw conclusions that eventually create our values and beliefs system. Then, we act according to the assumptions we've created. The thought process that goes that goes from observation happens at the subconscious level. It is repeated every when we encounter the stimuli.

In this article, the Peter Senge inference ladder is shown below;

Step 7

Actions

Step 6

Beliefs

Step 5

Conclusions

Step 4

Assumptions

Step 3.

Meanings

Step 2

Making sense of facts

Step 1

The Observation

The conclusions we draw generally reinforce our beliefs and, in turn, affect the information we decide to take from our experiences. This means that we'll disregard certain facts and instead focus on bathed facts that agree with our convictions. The conclusions we draw and the actions that follow are not objective, but instead biased since we allow our beliefs to influence what we perceive. That's why perception is subjective. Two individuals looking at the same scene will come to two completely different conclusions from it.

To avoid making faulty decisions, we can make use of an inference ladder. It allows us to go back to our assumptions and determine the way they impact our thinking and conclusions. When you return to the prior step, and then rethinking your conclusion, you are able to find loopholes in your reasoning and thinking and then review your assumptions and conclusions. We often make quick decisions and end up ignoring important information and making poor decisions.

Utilizing the ladder of inference will assist you with a rational reasoning process that will increase the effectiveness of your reasoning. It will also result in more informed choices.

To reduce the impact that our own beliefs have about the conclusions we draw, we should take a conscious effort to challenge our natural reactions through:

* Growing our levels of self-awareness, which is possible by taking time to examine our feelings as well as thoughts and the triggers that trigger them.

* Growing our levels of social awareness through being aware of and appreciate the perspectives of others, their emotions, and the attitudes of other people

Change our belief systems and forming new patterns of thought through the development of our own mental models are the best method of shaping our lives by our actions and behaviour. Psychological models are thoughts and concepts of thinking that can be applied to improve our abilities in thinking about solutions and coming up with ideas. They include:

Knowing your area of expertise

Each one of us, through the process of education, experience or talent has abilities and expertise in specific areas. Certain of us have talents in music or other arts while others excel in the field of chemistry. Our circle of expertise is made up of areas we excel both in a personal and a social level. Being aware of your capabilities specific to one particular field and the best method to utilize these talents is an essential aspect of your personal growth and success.

In the process of pursuing areas you're not skilled at can lead to anxiety, low self-confidence and a lack of motivation. Just as success leads to success, continuous failure may lead to lack of motivation and enthusiasm that can result in more failure. If you are finding that your efforts are constantly being unsuccessful, it could be time to reevaluate your competence circle with respect to your goals.

Self-awareness is the key to identifying the strengths as well as weaknesses. Knowing the things you excel in, areas you'd like to work on and what drives you are the most important factors needed for personal growth. Setting goals and objectives that reflect your strengths provides you with the chance to make the most of your talents and natural talents. Recognizing your area of expertise will help you to understand your the purpose of your life and provide you with a clarity on what to concentrate on and work towards.

First-principles of thinking.

The first principle approach to thinking is basically dissecting a process into its fundamental components and the concepts. First principles are an assumption that is fundamental and cannot be dismantled any further. It is about considering a situation from its base and beginning from the existing facts and starting from the basics.

If we can grasp the basic elements of a system, we can dismantle it and build it more efficiently. These fundamentals allow us to be averse to imitations and not relying on what has already been developed by others, but also allowing us to create your own system and conclusions by deconstructing the existing ideas and applying the fundamental elements to construct something completely new.

Inversion.

> All I want to know is where I will die so I do not go there.
> Charles Munger

Naturally, we want to think about what we wish to occur. If you'd like to become a doctor, you attend medical school, if you wish to run a marathon, you prepare your body to prepare for the race and it goes on. Inversion is to think about the goals you wish to accomplish in reverse, by focusing on the things you do not want to see occur.

If, for instance, you need to make a speech in public, you could think about the mistakes to avoid instead of focusing on how to make a decent speech. With this method it is easy to identify the issues that hinder you from delivering a great speech. If you are careful not to use the same language, or not conveying the right message, you may accidentally give a great speech simply by focussing on the things you shouldn't do.

By using this approach for making decisions and solving issues and problems, you will be able to effectively stop delay or find solutions that seemed beyond reach. When obstacles are eliminated and obstacles, we can clear the way to achieve the goal we have set.

Second-order thinking.

Thinking in second order requires that we look at your decisions, their immediate effects of these actions, and the long-term consequences that will be a consequence of the decisions you make. The question "and what if you don't?" influences second-order thinking.

In a scenario where you're torn between finishing your work or going out with your friends. If you are weighing the pros and cons of staying at home and writing your essay and going out with buddies to a bar, going out might be more enjoyable. If you think "and after that what" you are likely to discover that one of the options could have negative consequences.

Looking beyond the immediate results of a decision and focusing on the effects is essential to making decisions that last positive results and to ensure that we do not fall from our long-term goals.

Bayesian Method.

Bayesian method is Bayesian technique is statistical method based on theory which explains the degree of confidence in the possibility or occurrence of an incident. When applying this method to thinking, it the thought of considering every possible outcome and scenario. If we add new information to the existing probabilities and make them more current to make a more realistic assumption and make choices in the context of the expected results. The constant updating of our field of probabilities ensures that we can build more realistic simulations of possible scenarios and outcomes. This allows us to utilize this knowledge to make choices that are aligned with the outcome we want to achieve.

Mental simulations.

It is possible to use simulations to predict what might happen. Mental simulations help us in predicting possible outcome that we take. Through these simulations, we can make use of the conclusions made to decide the best way to proceed in any particular scenario. It is possible to use the mental model to not just forecast future events but also anticipate what might happen in the future.

Occam's razor.

The Occam's razor principle can be described as an approach to solving problems. It eliminates impossible options and argues that, in most cases the most straightforward explanation is usually the right one. It encourages us to concentrate on what is working and to not get bogged down in intricate theories. Spending time and energy thinking about complicated scenarios could be counterproductive and difficult. Making decisions based on simple reasoning and logical scenarios limit the margin of error. Occam's Razor principle is a good way to trust our instincts.

Hanlon's razor.

The concept of Hanlon's razor is based around focusing your thinking about finding solutions to the issue rather than focusing on finding the source of the problem or blaming someone else for the cause of the issue. If we apply this principle to our thinking process, we don't think that bad things are due to the fault of someone else, but instead to a lack of understanding. The time and effort we devote to the obsession with people who are to blame for problems implies that we don't look for the solution.

Important Mental Models for the Key Disciplines

Mind Models and Simulations within Physics

There are a variety of mental models in physics which are used in a variety of systems and are extensively used to other disciplines as well. They include:

It is the Law of Reciprocity.

This law of physics says that for every action , there will be a counter and equal reaction. This is a multidisciplinary law that can be found not only in the field of physics, but as well in human behavior, biology as well as many other fields. This law can be used to assess and make decisions taking the consequences of these choices in our minds.

It is an endless series or choices that we have to make every day. The sum of these choices determines our current behavior as well as our future actions. The choices that we make will have consequences in the short and in the long run. By applying our law of reciprocity it is possible to make more informed decisions by looking at what the consequences of our decisions will be over time.

Relativity.

The theory is applicable across different areas of the field of physics. The most popular concept in this law it is that a person is not able to fully comprehend a system in which they are a part.

A passenger in an airplane may not experience the movement of the plane, but an observer can be able to observe the movements that are taking place.

Similar to personal situations, when someone is caught in something or a situation and is unable to judge the situation from a neutral perspective since they are absorbed in the event and only view it from one angle. To be able to judge an event objectively it is necessary to first disengage our self from the mental aspect and observe it from an outsider's perspective.

Thermodynamics.

The law of thermodynamics is called"the law of conserving energy", and it describes the energy transfer in an entire system. The law states that energy can't be produced or destroyed within an environment, but simply moves from one form of energy to another.

Velocity.

Velocity is the measurement of speed in the particular direction or vector. The addition of a vector direction. Applying this concept to our lives can assist us to track our progress through various spheres. By having an established beginning point and ending point in terms of goals We can evaluate our performance. Knowing if you're progressing or not will assist in making adjustments to ensure that you're in the right direction to achieve your goals.

Catalysts.

Catalysts are an element that accelerates an chemical reaction while remaining independent of the reaction. Catalysts are found in every day life as well as in research. Finding catalysts we can apply in our daily life to help us accelerate the pace of progress and help us achieve our goals can assist us to achieve our goals and increase the speed that we can to reach these goals.

Leverage.

A lot of engineering innovations are based on the notion of leverage. Leverage is a concept which is employed to define methods by which heavy loads are lighter and, in turn, facilitate work.

Inertia.

The principle of inertia says that a body without net force acting upon it will either sit at rest or move in a uniform manner in an unidirectional line. Inertia is the fundamental physical principle that governs motion. Inertia helps to reduce energy use by limiting movement and actions.

Mind Models and Biology Biology

The laws of biology are applicable to all living organisms including single-celled living organisms like yeast to multi-cellular organisms, such as humans. The most important biological models include:

The Adaptation

To survive in their surroundings, the species of plants and animals need to change or die. Natural selection removes weaker species of an ecosystem, allowing the stronger species to live and reproduce. This natural process ensures that the next generation inherits the most effective genes from the gene pool.

The capacity to change and adapt to new situations and conditions is a crucial aspect of the human experience. The ability to adapt is an essential element for growth and success as change is a regular aspect of life. Our capacity to deal with it can ultimately affect our the personal growth of each person.

Chapter 4: Putting Mental Models In The Proper Perspective: What They Are And Not

Although mental models are certainly beneficial, they're not the keys of the kingdom' by themselves. Mental models are intended to help you get a clearer image of the reality. But, many people alter the picture by relying on their own personal experiences. While keeping information about our experiences is essential, it could cause bias. For a proper use of mental models, it's crucial that biases are recognized and compensated for. Otherwise the mental model will be just as flawed as the bias in it, making it difficult to accurately predict the outcome.

This section will help you understand the mental models and aren't that will allow you to determine how they could be utilized in real your daily life.

"We are all a part of mental models. They are the lenses through which we view the world, which determines our reactions to all that we encounter. Be conscious about your models in the mind is crucial to being neutral."

-Elizabeth Thorton

Mental models aren't completely reliable when it comes to their capacity to map out the world. They are susceptible to human error and do not always provide the full picture of the scenario. Once you're better aware of your mental model employ and the likelihood that they will produce either satisfying or unsatisfactory ideas, you can start selecting and deciding on the model you think is the most effective for the current situation. To do this it is essential to recognize the strengths of each model as well as the areas where it is weak.

As an example, suppose you had to solve a complicated maths problem. It is possible to go through hundreds of equations, however, without the correct equation used to solve the problem and the result was not an appropriate (or precise) solution.

Effects and Causes in Problem Solving

In many ways the human mind can be an enigma with two sides. Although it is quick to evaluate causes and effects however, this rapid evaluation frequently leads the mind to miss the most important factors. However, this doesn't mean that you don't have to think about and consider the millions of components that combine when you face a challenge or making a choice. But, it's important to consider a variety of factors that can significantly affect the outcome.

The primary advantage of this rapid causal-effect analysis that the mind does is that it establishes mental order and allows you to draw your conclusions in a rational manner which is logical. Although the brain's cause and effect model is like the mental model in its utility but it's also comparable to mental models in the sense that it's flawed. Cause-and-effect relations are a method of gaining insight and it's not unusual for them to be incorrect or misguided. The reasoning behind them is based upon the instincts and unconscious thought, not the logic (or the lack of rationality) of the circumstances.

Mindful Models

The most popular of Munger's theories on mental models are the notion that individuals can reduce the potential risks of an event by avoiding errors instead of trying to come the best solution. Even solutions that take a variety of variables into consideration could can expose someone to danger. In the end, no matter the person's talent the tendency they have to be risk-averse is bound cause them to have bad luck. It's not an issue of intelligence, but facts and statistics, and that there is no one person who is perfect every all the time. People naturally have blind spots. They are the result of connections, variables and other aspects which are easy to miss when a person doesn't notice them or doesn't have any experience with them.

When a person is aware of the blind spots inside the cognitive models they employ daily and can discern and recognize the blind areas. For instance, many people have confirmation bias. This is the tendency to select evidence based on the evidence that supports their beliefs instead of looking for the truth. When someone is aware of this tendency, they are able to examine the evidence more critically at the evidence and develop a more accurate and reliable mental model.

Mental Models can be useful or they can be limiting

One of the most difficult things when it comes to examining the tools within our toolbox is that we have a narrow perspective of our world. For instance, someone who is divorce lawyers might overanalyse the relationships they want to build because they observe divorce all over the place. Although this can be helpful in the identification of problems in a relationship but it also causes people to search for issues. If the divorce lawyer is always seeking out problems in their relationships, specifically those which have led to the death of some of their clients, they'll always be struggling to feel content in a relationship. They might find it difficult to be committed because they have so many commitments that fail day in and out.

For mental models to be effective they must be utilized in a manner that benefits. When it comes to divorce lawyers being constantly making excuses for problems to achieve to achieve their goal instead of recognizing the issue and using their expertise to tackle the issues, they will end up making the wrong choice and ending up with a failed dating experience. The most important thing to do when applying mental models effectively is to utilize them in a manner that will yield the most benefits with the least risk.

If you place two business executives and an environmentalist together and request them to talk about the best way to use the land they have The possibilities are numerous and it may be difficult for the two to reach a consensus on everything. The business person will likely be more focused on the ecosystem by looking at how it can be used for development or how it could make money in some way and the environmental expert could be interested in improving the natural habitat, or the overall quality of the environment.

Both could be at a crossroads because of what's called mental models. In simple terms they are depictions of our world. Mental models are used by people to help them solve their problems. They develop mental models over time as they discover new information and identify patterns throughout their lives.

The ability to master mental models is an excellent thing, but it can also have the potential to be a downside. People who are dependent on a few mental models or methods of thinking will ultimately hinder their ability to perceive the full potential of the scenario. It is difficult to pick the most optimal outcome since they don't perceive the real-world implications of the options in the front of them.

It's normal to have a preference for specific mental images, specifically after you've gotten used to thinking in a certain manner. However, the more you are a fan of a specific mental model the greater the likelihood that the model will end up being your fall. It's easy to fall trapped in choosing the mental models that are that are most familiar to you. When you're tackling issues or making decisions but the best outcome may not be the one that is at hand. If you let familiarity guide your decisions then it's almost impossible to make the necessary changes needed to achieve the best results. Keep in mind that while experience can be beneficial especially when setting yourself up as an authority in a particular subject, it could also be a drawback.

Removal of Bias From Mental Models

Mental models are extremely susceptible to bias. Much like attorney for divorce cases, these models only saw the negative aspects of the issues instead of looking for ways to correct the issues. The easiest method to get rid of bias is to focus on the facts.

data that is able to be verified. This can be difficult, especially when it comes to relationships with family members, as it is difficult to let go of emotion. This is especially applicable at work. Imagine that someone is offered the chance to take an entire week's trip with colleagues which could increase their career prospects. But, the person who is who is in charge of taking the vacation is one they don't enjoy working with. They might be biased in their choice of whether or not to go due to their relationship with the person to stand out of the way of achieving bigger goals in their lives. They are, however, penalizing themselves, rather than the person they are blaming and opting for a route that will result in a lower level of achievement.

To be successful in your life It is essential that you're open to new perspectives and thoughts. One of the biggest errors which people commit when sharing their ideas with other people or having disagreements is to not pay attention.

Instead of listening to opinions of the other and utilizing it to get a fresh perspective, they could block the idea before it is realized as they do not like hearing any ideas that are contrary to their convictions.

To make the most of the mental model, all of these mistakes have to be overcome. Learning is the most important aspect of using all mental models you have at your disposal. As you build connections between the concepts across various disciplines, you will gain more knowledge of the available information and various methods of thinking. Instead of avoiding this, it's important to accept it and stay open to new concepts and fresh perspectives. In the end, with more results, you have an increased likelihood of being successful.

What Mental Models are Not: A Continuous

Mental models are not an absolute state, since they are subject to change as new information or patterns are added in the. The primary purpose of mental models is to provide the illusion or representation of the world right in front of you. Most often, mental models are visually-based. By incorporating information into the "matrix" of known as a mental model outcomes of the model can change.

While mental models are utilized for decision-making and mental processes, they're not absolute by any means. Mental models are not without limitations in terms of the information available at the moment as well as the person's own perception of the circumstance they find themselves in, and limitations that are that are based in the mind model itself because there is no one mental model that is able to make conclusions or choices. It's all about selecting and deciding on which mental model are best suited to the specific scenario at hand.

It is not unusual to see terms like if and or to generate conditions in the mental model. These conditions permit scenarios to be played in its entirety and allows for concrete conclusion to be made. These terms also aid in determining the cause for the weaknesses and issues within mentally constructed models.

What is Mental Models are: tools to help you understand

Mental models are essential for understanding the world that surrounds us. The issue is that although the ideal scenario requires a tangle of various mental models, the reality is that things do not always work out as planned. The majority of people are experts that limit our capacity to make decisions based on those small mental models we are experts in. Psychologists can consider incentives in terms of motivations because they understand that individuals have motives for in the way they do. Engineers are systems thinkers and biologists consider the evolution of things and changes. The issue is that by just looking at the issue from one viewpoint, you create an unblind spot that makes it impossible for the issue to be seen in its entirety and to realize its potential.

The issue is that, with only a few mental models it is not possible to comprehend the entire scope of something without being able to recognize different mental models. Imagine that a team of people were assigned the responsibility of managing a forest that was dying. Business people will only consider the worth of the area and whether they should modify it to suit their needs instead of seeking to save its natural environment. Environmentalists may be concerned about the impact of climate change. However, botanists would focus on the entire ecosystem and the impacts of the various animals and plants that inhabit the region. Forestry engineers can only consider the forest in terms of the growth of trees. If they are not able to share information, however each one of them are unable to discern the forest and are unable to find the best solution. The best solution is for all disciplines to be able to share their mental models which would allow them to be able to see the whole view and develop the most complete solution.

Charlie Munger explored this idea in a speech from the 1990s, in which he summarized the concept of mental models as well as the concept to practical wisdom. He stated that the primary principle is that it's not enough to be able to recall specific facts. It's almost impossible to recall a sequence of facts, particularly since wisdom doesn't come from the person who remembers the most information. Wisdom is the result of collecting the facts and putting them up on a latticework of theory in order to produce an acceptable shape. Without models, simply recollecting facts will be useless.

The application of the Mental Models

When you read the article, you must keep in mind that while the ability to master a variety of models is beneficial but it's not enough to simply keep a list of mental models. Mental models have limitations. They're not some magic formula that will lead you to success in your life. Along with being aware of the biases of others, you must learn how to apply different mental models to generate fresh outcomes. When you are able to determine the mental models that are suitable for your work and daily life, make the time to research different scenarios and the mental models that could be used to these situations. Through studying the numerous ways in which mental models may be utilized, you equip yourself with the knowledge of numerous applications. While there are some that are only applicable in specific fields but many models can be adapted and utilized to make more effective, suitable decisions in other areas of our lives as well.

Chapter 5: What Are Your Mental Models? And How Can They Influence Your Behavior?

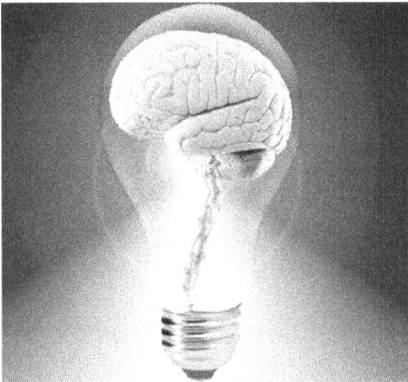

In order to begin this discussion and examine the specific motives and implications behind it I'd like to offer a quick review: Do you have any behaviors that you don't like about yourself, but are unable to change? How often have you been into situations in which you'd like to do things differently? Have you ever thought about why it's so hard to alter your the way you behave, even though it is harmful to you in some way? Our behavior is closely tied to our beliefs, and they frequently influence our ways of thinking and acting and causing us to react following a set of rules we've been taught.

You may, for instance, believe that being late is a sign of disrespect. of respect. That's why you develop the attitude of being punctual. The author Peter Senge, in The Fifth Discipline described mental models to be "deeply established beliefs, generalizations, images and stories that impact our ways of thinking about the world and acting upon the basis of it." A mental model may not be absolute and is instead a construct by your own convictions, that is, the beliefs you hold that influence your actions. The mental models we use determine not only the way we view the world around us, but also how we behave within it.

Another fascinating fact is that when faced with the same scenario, different individuals can react differently which is directly connected to mental model each person has. Understanding a mental model and then bringing it to the forefront isn't an easy feat however it is essential to know how we are affected by this way of thinking, which is, how often we perform certain actions in various circumstances. It is crucial to be aware how the mental models could be limiting or pushing us towards goals or personal identity.

The development of the best mental models that can be used to tackle every situation that arises is the most important aspect to maximize the effectiveness of development and learning. Two abilities can aid in the process of discovering mental models such as reflection and inquiry. Reflecting refers to being aware of the ways that mental models influence our understanding of the world. Likewise "inquiring" refers to maintaining conversations and interactions with others by sharing experiences and visions.

Reflection can help bring the mental model into consciousness, and a little questioning can help to determine if it is the right mental model to employ for the moment. If the mental model is limiting or helps you reach your goals.

Mental Models and Decision Processes

It is now clear what is a mental model! Right? Yes, you're right. It is our system of internal representations. It's the way we view the world in relation to factors like the way we feel, our life experiences, and our culture. Over time we develop ideas that shape the way we'll be able to experience the future or view the world around us.

The mental models that we have developed also have a distinct influence on decision making. It's like we have recorded our patterns of behaviour and concepts that we have used in the analytical process that we've created. We are programmed to situations in a specific manner. This is beneficial since it accelerates the selection of an option. It is a matter of what happens when our mental models are not as efficient as they used to be?

Mental Renewal

A quick question: Is it a good idea to maintain rigid behavior in the event of a change? With regard to the decisions we make our mental models need to be in line with our requirements and obligations. That means our priorities when deciding could change based on the circumstance and situation we face.

This way, without any dynamism, we are at the danger of reverting to outdated mental models. It's dangerous to choose what we should do in the near future by looking back at the past. After all, as with almost everything in life, what is great today could be outdated one day.

Mental Models to the practice

Imagine you spent five years in the field of computer technician in the largest infrastructure company. The workload was enormous and you were accountable for just about everything, including in areas that were not part of your formal training. You'd do your job make your invoices, make new business enquiries and then take care of the events that occurred.

As time passed, you began into the belief that you had to take care of everything, comprehend the entire process in detail and not delegate your duties to anyone. In essence, for five decades, you have been trained to believe that you were a certain way and believed that that was your role in the company.

One day you were promoted. You were made an Infrastructure Project Manager. You no longer manage the technical aspect of a project anymore however everyone has to answer to you. Tell me about your increasing obligation of looking after all the details, being accountable for all things and managing everything yourself, do they still applicable? Generally, no. It's fine when you are looking to get wild.

A new mental model became necessary, delegating. Remaining in the mindset that were prevalent in the era of technicians will render your new model impossible to achieve. The new decisions can no longer be made based on the interpretation of the world in the same way as it was before.

Renew your life and make it a habit

The effects of changes can create imbalances either positive or negative. We often fight against the imbalance in order to get back to a steady state. So, the application of mental models is a counter-response to the changes that we encounter in every aspect in our daily lives.

Recognize those mental images, and determine whether they're appropriate for the present and make changes whenever needed. Don't be a slave to models and always work on to change the way you view the world. Revising your understanding of facts could be the difference lines between failure and success.

Chapter 6: Upgrade Your Thinking

When I first read the 1995 Charlie Munger Speech, The Psychology of Human Misjudgment it became clear that I would gain much more than I did from my MBA. Then I spent the following couple of years studying and learning about cognitive biases, and how we can fool ourselves. Munger proved to him that this world has many more things to provide than business and computer science which were the two fields I'd been spending long periods of time. He opened up a whole world of mental models. This is a fancy term that refers to the tools of thinking that you can utilize to solve issues.

The mental model an image of how something operates. We are unable to store all the details of life within our brains, therefore we employ models to reduce the complicated into manageable and manageable chunks. We are aware of it and/or not, we employ these models each day to make decisions, think and comprehend our world.

Although there exist millions of models for your mind available, I'd like to focus on nine models that can assist you in thinking better.

1. The Map isn't the Territory

The map of reality isn't the reality. Even the most accurate maps aren't perfect. They are merely reductions in the way they present. If a map could depict the entire territory with complete accuracy, it would not be a reduction, and it would not be useful for us. Maps can also represent a snapshot of the past which represents something that is no longer in existence. This is an important thing to keep in mind when we think through issues and take better choices.

2. Circle of Competence

If ego and not competency dictate our actions we are blind. If you are aware of the basics and know what you are doing, you will be able to tell which areas you are able to stand over your peers. If you're transparent about what you know and where it is lacking, you will know which areas you're weak and what you can do to improve. Knowing what your competence circle is enhances decisions and the outcomes.

3. The First Principles Thinking

Thinking from the first principles is among the best methods to reverse-engineer complex situations and unlock creative possibilities. Sometimes referred to as reasoning from the fundamental principles, it's an instrument to aid in resolving complex issues by separating the basic notions or facts from the beliefs based on them. What's left are the basic facts. If you are familiar with the basic foundations of something, you can build your knowledge on them to make something entirely that is completely new.
4. Think Play

Thought experiments are defined as "devices of the imagination utilized to study how things."[1A variety of disciplines, like Physics and philosophy utilize thinking experiments to explore the things that can be discovered. Through this, they could open new avenues for exploration and inquiry. They are effective because they allow us to discover our mistakes and avoid repeat ones. They allow us to take on the impossible, analyze the possible outcomes of our choices, and revisit our history to make better choices. They will help us determine what we truly need, and the most effective method to achieve it.

5. Second-Order Thinking

Nearly everyone is able to anticipate the immediate effects from their decisions. This kind of thinking is safe and easy however it's also an opportunity to make sure you'll receive exactly the same results that all others get. Second-order thinking involves thinking further ahead and thinking more holistically. It is a requirement to consider not just our actions and the immediate effects they have, but also the consequences that follow these actions too. Not taking into consideration the third and second-order effects could create disaster.

6. Probabilistic Thinking

Probabilistic thinking is basically looking to determine, with certain mathematical tools and logic the probabilities of a certain outcome happening. It's among the most powerful tools available to increase the precision of our choices. In a world where every event is motivated by an inexplicably complicated set of variables and variables, probabilistic thinking allows us to determine the most likely results. If we can identify these the probabilities, our decisions are more precise and efficient.

7. Inversion

Inversion is an effective method to enhance your thinking since it assists you in identifying and remove obstacles to your success. The essence of inversion lies in the word "invert," which means to flip upside down. In terms of a tool for thinking, it is the process of approaching a problem by looking at it from the opposite side of the initial point of origin. We tend to consider an issue that is forward. Inversion lets us turn the problem around and consider it in reverse. Sometimes , it is best to begin from the beginning, however it's sometimes more beneficial to start at the top.

8. Occam's Razor

Simple arguments are much more likely be correct than more complicated explanations. This is the basic premise of Occam's Razor which is a well-known concept of logic and solving problems. Instead of trying to debunk complex scenarios You can make your decisions with greater confidence by relying on an most straightforward explanation with the smallest number of moving components.

9. Hanlon's Razor

In its difficult to pinpoint the source of its inspiration It is believed that Hanlon's Razor declares that we shouldn't blame malice for something that can be explained more easily through stupidity. In a complicated world the use of this model can help us to stay clear of ideology and paranoia. In general, by not assuming that the failures result from the person who is doing the wrong thing We look for alternatives instead of ignoring opportunities. This approach shows us that we all make mistakes. It is imperative to inquire whether there's a better explanation for the circumstances that took place. The most likely explanation to be true is one that has minimum intention.

Improve your decision-making

Mental models are the frameworks that offer people an idea of the way in which the world operates. They enable you to see the world from different perspectives and aid in identifying solutions to problems that could be outside of your realm of knowledge. Every person has their own method to look at the world and the perception of people's surroundings (or anything else) is based on their beliefs, knowledge as well as their experiences and views as a result is influenced by the person's economic, political, and cultural background. Sometimes, looking through a lens can help make things clearer and can help people come closer to making the right choice.

Mental models help us think outside of our personal experiences. They can also provide an underlying conceptual "shortcut," making it simpler, quicker and more efficient to solve issues. Albert Einstein said, "To break an intellectual model is much more difficult than breaking the atom." The process of defining the concept of a mental model in this broad manner has implications for the application or understanding. Phillip Johnson-Laird (a professor of Princeton's Department of Psychology) pointed to the fact that every mental model is just one of a variety of models that can be utilized in a specific context.

Our brains are extremely adept at constructing conceptual models that represent our current physical world. The problem becomes more complex when we begin thinking in terms of abstractions. Sometimes, we are able to recognize a problem and if we can see it within the context in which we were taught it, we'll recognize it. However, when we look at it in a different setting it is possible that we will not be able to recognize it. This implies that "two individuals who have different mental models may witness the same event and explain it differently since they've experienced different elements."

To begin to identify the issues to make better decisions, you must change the approach to your problem by replacing heuristics with long-term goals by utilizing strategic methods to improve your results. Be aware of your actions and the reason you're doing it. Try to avoid making mistakes by identifying your blind areas.

What are blind spots?

There are blind spots everywhere and weakness that we must address. Get rid of blind spots to make problem-solving easier. One good example of this could be power plants in comparison to. environmentalists.

Power plants are a facility that generates electricity with the aid from one or several generators that convert various sources of energy into electricity by using the primary sources of energy like coal. It releases a lot of carbon dioxide over it's life. An environmentalist sees the negative impact on climate change as a result of the pollutant emissions caused by power plants powered by coal that are linked to asthma as well as lung and heart illnesses, neurological issues pollution from acid rains, climate change as well as other serious environmental and health effects. When you view the issue from two perspectives each of them is incorrect, however neither of them can develop an effective plan over the long term which will benefit everyone. Knowing the basics of other disciplines could result in a more flexible understanding , which would enable more informed decisions in the beginning.

The above example is connected close to the two main biases: Hindsight bias and Confirmation bias. Both are key to the way people view things.

What are Hindsight and Confirmation Biases? And How Can They hinder our ability to draw the right conclusions?

Confirmation In Mental Models The mind sees the things they prefer to perceive and ignore the rest. They prefer evidence that supports their previous beliefs and omit evidence that doesn't conform. When given facts and facts, we usually choose those that we believe best suits us regardless of whether they're true or not.

It is believed that the British Government was first in the world to employ onboard radars to identify enemy aircrafts. Whatever the darkness was outside, Royal Air Force pilots were in a position to detect planes in their displays and then shoot them down. The enemy did not know that the British could have their planes snooping around in the night sky, but to the British it was a technological advancement that won them war. They were not willing to let go of their technology, therefore the best option was to deceive. They devised a campaign which linked eating carrots to greater vision. It was a bogus science however... this did the trick. Both British as well as the Germans believed in it, and interestingly, we still believe it a full 75 years after.

Hindsight Bias In Mental Models

Hindsight bias is the tendency to view events that have already taken place as being more likely to occur than they were prior to their happening. They can help us become not as accountable for our actions as well as being less critical about ourselves and confident enough to make the right decisions.

This is a real illustration. When people have a wrong idea regarding the outcomes of an event, they say they knew that it would go in differently than they had originally said. It is usually heard during a wedding ceremony, " I knew it since the first time I saw them and they were intended to get married." However, the moment separation occurs and the same person is able to be back to say, "The signs were there but they didn't see it ahead of time."

When you're a spectator, most of the time you'll find yourself just ignoring the person, and letting them make another mistake instead of notifying them of the mistake. If this mistake is not pointed out or noticed by anyone is likely to result in a life of routine.

Charles Duhigg, an author of "The Power of Habit," stated that" habits do not come into existence but are created. Every good, bad or even insignificant habit begins with a mental pattern known as"habit loop. "habit loop." Habit-forming and breaking are closely related. The commitment (a personality characteristic) and a plan (what you contribute to the circumstance) are the most important factors.

Habits are habits that we perform with almost subconscious regularity. Psychologists define them as a habitual way of feeling, thinking or a desire that is acquired by repetition. Habits we develop every day can lead us to achievement or prevent us from getting there. Do challenges and difficulties stop you from working towards your goals? If so, there's an explanation. Continue to work hard and you will see success.

In 2009 Phillippa Lally, Cornelia H. M. van Jaarsveld, Henry W. W. Potts and Jane Wardle examined the process of forming habits in daily life. They recruited 96 people who picked one of the following: drinking, eating, or activity habit that they would carry out every day within the same setting during 12 weeks. After sixty-six weeks, the simple routine was in place and operating on autopilot. But , as the study shows it could take for as long as an eight-and-a-half months to allow more complex habits to develop.

Another excellent illustration is the 21-day period of the task completion study. In the 1960's Psycho-Cybernetics book, Maltz, a plastic surgeon, observed that his patients took approximately 21 days to get adjusted to their new looks. Maltz didn't find any evidence that 21 days of work completion becomes a habit.

To modify habits and build new structures, loop learning is essential.

From the standpoint of learning in organizations The development of a an ability to sustainably learn of (key components of) the company is an essential requirement for survival and success in ever-changing and challenging environments. Learn more about this research paper published by Maastricht University. Maastricht University, Faculty of Economics and Business Administration, on circular organizing and triple loop learning.

What can we do to Make Our Experiences Better?

* Lean from our own experiences make use of the checklist

Learn from other people's experiences, either through listening or by communicating

• Read - Find inspirational books, podcasts, etc.

Make a list of your mental models, whether harmful or constructive, and record them down.

* Constructive thought refers to various higher-order mental processes which are involved in the development of, updating, and maintaining of representations in the brain of the world outside.

* Creative Destruction refers to the process that results in perpetual turnover, which sees the development of new and improved concepts, products, processes and businesses take over (destroy) old ones. - Don't get outdated

Chapter 7: Critical Thinking

How do you define critical thinking?

There's a phrase that evokes many different opinions. The academic community might interpret the phrase in a certain way, whereas your instructor could present it in a different manner, however, you could consider something different completely. In this article I'll be looking at what this could mean about children. You are constantly developing, day-to day changing, explorative, curious and into everything, requires constant stimulation to learn and grow whether you are a child or a little girl.

The elements of critical thinking include assessment, perception and judgment, making an inference, and solving. Critical thinking can also be described as the capacity to think in a unique way while coming up with accurate conclusions.

How often in a day could be considered a day to be unobservant, trying to make a little effort of living? If an issue arises it can be a source of irritation.

Why?

Imagine a scenario in which you encountered a problem and, as it arose that you looked at it in a different way. Imagine a scenario where you took it as an opportunity to think about what had occurred and consider the possibilities that particular problem could be solved.

Do you need to be an imaginative person to be able of thinking critically? I'm not sure. I am of the opinion that we, as a group can come up with solutions to problems. I am of the opinion that even as a child, using puzzles, building squares and riddles physical and mental puzzles, even perusing them, can stimulate the mind to lock in. Even fantasies are beneficial when the child is exposed to an unfamiliar situation, yet has shown that the result is positive.

Critical thinking is a process that can, in the end, it can also increase ingenuity. The act of looking at another idea, evaluating it and deciding on an innovative arrangement is an essential element of developing your child's critical thinking abilities.

Being able to observe and analyze - making an assessment, and then ultimately making your own conclusions are crucial steps to fixing any problem. To accomplish this it is best to be thinking ahead, analyze "consider the possibilities" and decide which will be the best method of achieving the goal. The importance of teaching our children to think strategically isn't to be undervalued. A majority of kids live in the present, in the current time and space. A majority of kids don't put aside the effort to look into the future. In a way, given the amount of sexting happening, today's teenagers aren't. I'm sure that if these teenagers had been taught certain critical thinking-forms earlier they could have been able to consider their choices and decide the consequences - "Goodness it's likely that this won't be a good idea."

The ability to discern between fact and opinion can be easily identified with the ability of a person to think critically. Perhaps that's why many people today are swayed by the rhetoric of our politicians instead of deciding the best option for themselves.

The Critical Scholars are the practitioners.

Supporters can be once in an era a scholar of critical thinking. It's not a lot of effort to follow someone before you. Your feet connect and move. How often did your mother say, "If Tommy hopped off a ladder, would you attempt the same?" Naturally, you replied "No! " However how many of our children currently are just following to their hero - fantastic or awful?

The world is changing rapidly. Perhaps you remember the days when the typical family had one TV and one phone, as well as one car. At no time, dreamed of the web, an PC as well as an iPhone. If your child isn't able to swiftly progress in this constantly changing world, they will be forced to seek out. As a group require our children to be innovators, but they must be pioneers in a positive way.

We, as a society, have proven to be a lot centered on the rules. The study halls of today are firmly inclined towards rules. Our public is a part of the law's victims. At present I'm not saying it's not right. The need for rules and laws is a necessity of our existence as humans. However the rigid rules are the reason why our children are getting out of the realm of critical thinking. Should Benjamin Franklin had pursued the rules could he have created the power? In the event that Alexander Graham Bell had not had conceived of a problem and later attempted to resolve the issue, would we still be using the phone? No! It is "out from the bottle" thinking. There were no reference points.

There were no guidelines for the issues they were trying to solve. They, like all the remarkable creative minds of their time employed their critical thinking abilities that were more advanced in their thinking and thinking skills and were "fresh" and took the proper path to develop and create.

In the midst of all the state-mandated exams that are now being administered in the study halls, we are merely "rememberers," But rememberers are not able to remember for very long. Perhaps the child who was encouraged to think about the answer, that question or event, and then end their thinking processes (critical thought) will be able to recall that answer in a very significant duration.

Kids love to respond to questions (in all instances, they do when they're young people , but not necessarily!). As a parent can create a space that your child's critical thinking processes are boosted.

A baby's reaction to the most abstract concept as "imagination." Ask your child "Where are you imagining?" "What is your imagination doing?" Go through a book and explain that the author's imagination crafted the story. Later the story was recorded for you to read. Inspire your child to consider the story. Write it down in case your child is mature enough to allow him to think it through.

Pose questions. Unorganized, no formal test/answers questions, but informal conversations. You can play the "imagine the scenario that you imagine" game. Questions that begin by "consider the possibility" will lead to informal conversations with your child. These discussions don't simply serve as a powerful holding tool however, it also acts to allow your child an opportunity to fully consider your position of view, formulate the reasoning behind it and come to with a conclusion. Don't be quick to make judgments. There aren't any wrong or incorrect answers . It's just the response of your child - that was based on by his growing critical thinking abilities. The importance of having fun in the company of your child is not or, as I see it, overemphasized.

The old adage "give an individual fish and he'll be able to eat this day, but show the fisherman how to fish and he'll have a feast for the rest of his life" sounds like a bell. Place your child (alone) on the dining table and read the book on his lap or sit down with him with the book. Peruse. Discuss. Consider. Play.

Which of the two was more well-reacted?

When their thinking abilities develop as they develop, your child will become acquainted with the tasks of situations and the logical outcomes and, as a result the selflessness and the reasonableness. They'll be able to make a distinction between right from improper and develop trustworthiness that they can carry to adulthood.

Soon you will be seeing the skills being used more often, because once your mind is locked it's like being a snowball that is that is sliding downwards. Get out of the way. Your child is unstoppable!

I'll let you know Sir Isaac Newton's law of latency "an object that is moving will continue to be moving until it is followed on by an outside force" and the reverse around "a book that is in rest will remain in place until it is followed on by an outside force."

However, on the other side I would like to declare: A brain in rest will remain at rest until it is followed by an ingenuous parent.

Critical Thinking Skills are essential. Skills

Critical thinking abilities are at an all-time level in the US. In both public and private settings the majority of the population is not equipped to intelligently and clearly thinking through the issue or challenge. What exactly is critical thinking? Although the meanings of critical thinking could be altered, an important aspect of the definition is to make use of reason, participation and expertise to analyze and articulate the problem. Also, to evaluate the quality of information and reach out to an informed, solid judgment answer.

Imagine that you're one of your students looking to research the American Civil War. The teacher informs her that it started in 1861 and was over by 1865. It was 1865. South used slaves. The North did not. The war was fought in order to hold the Union as a unit and also to liberate slaves. When the war, over 600,000 people had gone. The teacher, at this moment, instructs the student to be aware of these facts for the purpose of a test. Another teacher informs students about the preface that paves the way for war, possibly focusing on the issue of including the slave states as well as free states in the Union.

Furthermore, they might be discussing the rights that states needed to be successful as well as the fact that many countries were not able to be a part of the Union without this right to withdraw. It is also possible to mention that the liberation of slaves didn't become a reality until the war was just beginning. When they arrive in the aftermath of providing the student the information and the possibility of getting more information without any other person they will suggest that the student provide an honest, conscious assessment, and then make their own conclusions. Principal teacher promotes purposeful publicity, and the other is trying to foster critical thinking in the pupil.

The way we live here in the US has produced a society who is content with bite-sized news, superficial investigation and a superficial interest. Insufficient understanding and critical thinking issues typically leads to an easily control and lead populace. Many people are able to knowingly accept information given to them without little or no analysis. The so-called Elites are becoming more focused on retaining control, which means they're within a particular conviction system. This is the reason why that people from both ends of the political spectrum must fight to prove it clear that they own most of their Liberties and have acces to all information (this is not a valid excuse for National Security information). The control of the dissemination and availability of information is how the gossip elitists maintain the control and increase their capabilities. This is why that a limited government and gradually closer government are important. The less the government is connected with the lives of people and the more near it is located and the greater chance that people have to influence the course of change. In turn, citizens will utilize their critical thinking abilities frequently and the resulting sharp and rational choices will result in a more well-educated and better informed nation.

How do Mental Models let you access your brain

It's no problem to say "be more cautious" or "practice more critical thinking" but how exactly do you go about doing it? Where do you need to master critical thinking? Skepticism and learning aren't a part of studying history. It's not a whole lot of dates, facts or concepts. It's a process of uncertainty and critical thinking is something you practice. The best method to master the concepts of critical thinking and skepticism is to do them... but in order to master them you must learn the skills. How can you break free of this rut?

LEARN the basics: LOGIC, ARGUMENTS, FALLACIES

Skepticism may be a part of the process. It's an action that is based on certain principles on what constitutes great and poor thinking. There's no substitute to the basic knowledge, and if believe you've got all of the basic concepts, that is probably a great indication that you should examine them.

In fact, even professionals who deal with logic for a living can be misguided! There is no need to know more than an expert, however there's such a vast variety of fallacies that are able to be used from different perspectives there are bound to be those that you're not acquainted with. Additionally, there are ways these fallacies could be employed that you've not yet encountered in the present.

Don't assume you know everything. Instead, acknowledge that there is an extensive amount of work to do and set a goal to regularly review the various ways that fallacies are used and how logic-based arguments are constructed, and so on. There are always new ways to manipulate arguments so you need to keep up-to-date with the arguments they're making.

Practice THE BASICS

It's not enough to know about the fundamentals; you have to apply the information you've learned. It's like learning about a particular language in books but not using it. You'll never meet someone who is working in that language. The more you utilize logic and the rules of doubt, the better you'll accomplish it.

Making logical arguments is an easy and adroit method of achieving this. However, a much better option is to examine the arguments of other people since this will show you which actions to take and how to not do it. The editorial page of your newspaper is a great place to find out about the new topics. The letters to the editor , as well as "proficient" editorials, which contain a lot of terrible errors and fundamental flaws. If you aren't able to spot the slightest error on a random day, it's time to examine the entire document more closely.

Recall: THINK ABOUT WHAT YOU'RE THINKING

If you can get to the core of the issue and you can spot a flaw without thinking about it, which is a feat, but you shouldn't stop contemplating the things you're doing. The opposite is stated One of the indications of sound criticism and skepticism is the fact that the skeptical thinks deliberately and with a purposeful thinking, and even critically thinking. This is called a general-purpose.

Skepticism isn't only about being skeptical of people around you However, you also have the choice of developing an attitude of skepticism regarding your own ideas and assessments, as well as your tendencies and the ends. If you're looking to build this, you must be accustomed to taking your time to think about your ideas. There and then it could be more ardent than learning about the logic of things, yet it compensations across a variety of different areas.

Another word

The first thing to remember is that one of the most essential aspects of thinking critically is assessing your issue and the credibility of your information and the source. Before you proceed by taking the time to look at your issue it is essential to have reliable and accurate facts. If you can, a range of sources is recommended to aid in gaining perspective.

You will then need to solve your issue by using your intelligence and experiences. It sounds simple, but this is where many people diverge without putting their trust in their own judgment. A majority of people give the most trust to the opinions of others and ideas. Trust your own wisdom and experiences. Every person is a voice within that must be believed in.

Don't be afraid to utilize other individuals' perspectives and experiences but take a moment to think about it, while considering other aspects and trusting your gut instincts. The biggest issue in the development of critical thinking isn't in the hard analysis or a meaningful piece of information, they doubt the person. Unfortunately, many people feel uneasy about their abilities and knowledge. If you're younger and have a tendency to lean more toward reliable sources, while those who are older, lean more toward your skills and knowledge. At the end of the day, be whatever you want to be trust yourself, the innate wisdom of a person and logic as well as sound judgment are more solid than they realize.

In conclusion, you'll be required to continue to work in the direction of improving your ability to think critically about problems both small and large. over time your skills will greatly improve, which will have positive effects on your life. Remember, improving your critical thinking skills are similar to other skills, the more you work on it, the more sharp it becomes.

The Mental Model and the Active

There are likely to be individuals who are the embodiment of the perfect oblivious teacher. They're the ones...They cannot remember details or formulas, and they know less names of people and must refer to data that other people believe should be natural and consistent. But, as it happens when these supposed distracted individuals look at the information they require, they possess the ability to transform extremely complex ideas into easy-to-understand formulas or even words. They're the rational thinkers those who create discoveries, products or inventions. They're the Einstein thinkers of the world.

When asked the reason he had trouble remembering formulas, and also why he got low marks at high school Einstein replied, "I do not mess up my brain with facts. I can get up to speed on any standard source within about two minutes." Instead of wasting energy by recollection, Einstein took those effectively attained facts and created an entirely new discovery with them. He saw the connections between the results and the patterns that underlie the process. Similar to this, Einstein, who bombed math, helped us harness the particle, and eventually create an atomic force.

The current most creative leaders are in a lot of ways Einstein. Although they might have difficulties in determining clearly, precisely planned, what they are doing or re-creating their actions on paper they are asked to manage business, they can boast of a massive success. They can identify patterns that drive successful processes and apply these patterns to diverse and new businesses and achieve remarkable results everywhere they travel.

5 Different Types of Leaders

There aren't many genuine, Einstein thinkers. Perhaps, they are likely to be classified as one of four categories.

* The rational thinkers: They are able to learn from the data. They must investigate data in order before making the conclusion. In the absence of the hard data, they won't be able to proceed. In addition, without the data they won't be able to tell others how to make the necessary advancements.

* The verbal thinkers These individuals learn by listening. They are becoming more apt to apply. They are able to process the information they acquire and process it. But, even though they understand the same processes as other people do but re-creating the same process in another area is not easy for them.

The thinkers who use pictures They learn through observation. If you can graphically demonstrate to them how to do something, they'll accomplish it. If they have to follow directions without images, or even instructions which are extremely elegantly written the problem is lost. They are able to create stunning Atom models. However, they're not able to perform the calculations to tell you what the outcome will be.

Chapter 8: Think Differently Than Others

The primary and most evident differentiator between you and everybody else on this planet is that no one is developed exactly like you. Your body isn't identical to anyone else who has lived before or has ever lived - different in every aspect.

There is no one on the planet who can comprehend things the way you do. Nobody can create sentences the way you do, or reacts to these words in the same manner you respond to them. You are the only one with your own distinctive way of interpreting people locations, things words, events, and even the weather.

Let me provide you with a good example When you hear a baby crying and you respond, it is contingent on whether you're mommy of that baby or an innocent passerby. A mother may experience an underlying sense of criticality and will make a move, while the bystander is likely to remain in the same spot.

This is because Every person has an elevated perspective and has a wide range of implications, and gives distinct qualities to each scenario they face. We ought to take a look at each one of those.

Your perspective: You are and different from others because of your particular point of view. No one sees things from an identical perspective to what you do. The most famous example of this is visually impaired people experiencing various parts from an animal. Everyone believes his interpretation is correct and the other are off base. All are correct but not all are right. It's all about the perspective.

This means that you are unique in your thinking and stand out from others because you give the highest importance to particular things. In every town square around the globe the presence of an image of a cross (the symbol of Christianity) or an Star of David (the image of Judaism) or the sickle moon (the symbol of Islam) could each cause a very unexpected response from those who see them with regard to their changing meanings that they assign to each symbol.

Qualities: You are unique because of your circumstances. The things you observe or experience is deemed to be lucky or unlucky or a sandstone, important or not, obnoxious or attractive, dangerous or safe, enjoyable or exhausting, etc. depending on the qualities you possess that are derived from your ethics and beliefs, religious practices as well as social class, ethnicity, and so on.

Does this mean you've got your reality and I am the one who has my reality? Absolutely not! You can believe that the earth's level as well as that Elvis is still alive, if you wish to but that doesn't make it true. You may "feel" that something ishappening, but emotions aren't a reliable indicator of anything other than emotions. Even if you can observe something, it doesn't give it a straightforward. If you ask three witnesses to an auto accident to reveal the details of what happened and each of their versions will differ slightly, but there's only one exact and complete account of what took place.

In the case of intuition, your thoughts are yours and your discerning abilities are unique to you. This is why it is important to trying to test your judgement using factual information, and comparing the features and implications with the world around you, and be open at the chance of confusion. In addition, the most important thing is to keep in mind that our natural tendency is always to look things the way you want to.

The most effective way to be different in business is to think differently.

In order to hit gold in business, you must consider gold. What's your company's focus? What are you hoping to do to improve your profits? Here are some tips regarding the most efficient approach to be creative within the business:

Take note of what's in store

Don't wait until the devastating business storm strikes your company Instead, you should always think about the next steps to take or what you can do to improve. For instance what are the elements you must set up to ensure that your business grows? Which stage is your company at in relation to the outline of your business or in areas of growth or decline? Does your business plan align with the vision you have set for yourself? What is your current total income? What is the proposed total tax rate? What can you do to increase your profits? Reviewing your business's performance keeps you well-prepared for the future.

Make sure your ideas are profitable.

Always remember that your glass is half full. Think about the possible outcomes, not only probable requirements. As a business owner, you should maintain the positive mindset; believe that everything will go according to plan. There are risks that could be a concern and gadgets are designed to stay clear of or control the dangers. The risks aren't anticipated, but you can be prepared to maintain the distance and take care of the pressure. In business, being confident allows you to take a chance with yourself, to be determined to step risky and be confident that you're gaining respect, regardless of what the numbers say that they are generally. This is a method to think differently when it comes to business.

You can go beyond your current contributions

Do not just look at things superficially. Consider your options and conduct thorough research on the different ways your company can benefit from your target market. Think about the essential elements of your company's position at the moment. What are your current business issues? Define them and break them so that you can see the ways you can make an impact. Draw a diagram of your SWOT analysis for business (Strengths weaknesses, strengths openings, weaknesses, and threats). Be more than the surface; think about the implications.

Your competitors are watching.

Know your company's needs and be familiar with the processes of your rivals If you're not, you could bet that your rivals are working hard. What do they have that perform better than yours? What can you do to influence them to collaborate and cooperate to obtain the most important assets? What's the most effective method to increase generosity? Conduct a research on your business and keep an eye on the events that occur in your company circumstances. This is business, so you must make sure you are prepared to face the challenges. It's all about benefit-making and charity, so be focused around these goals.

Create a war room

Because you know who your competitors are and are aware of the nature of your business. Make sure you distinguish the risks and evaluate the risks. Comparing your business with your closest rival. Prepare for battle. Make a spreadsheet of your benefits and deals. Does your company have the ability to survive to a downturn in business or a volatile economy? Find out how you can improve your business? What's not working? Do your key personnel perform exactly as they should? Do you have an evaluation of your exhibition. Do something to make the necessary improvements to your business and run a few advertisements and up your game in business. Remember that it's an exchange of benefits and that should be the focus.

You can pound your chest

What makes you unique is what makes you exceptional. Develop your business skills and improve it. Every item or administrative process should have its distinctness, the thing that makes it different from the same as the other. Gadget will help you make your business's goals and goals unique. The uniqueness of Gadget is the quality that shows how your company is similar to your competitors, yet different in the areas of idea, marking and product contribution.

There is no business without its advantages. The seed of a business can grow when the soil for business is fertile and the wealth comes with your business concerns. Make deductions more effective in a way that is unexpected.

11 Tips For The Mental Health Care Reform

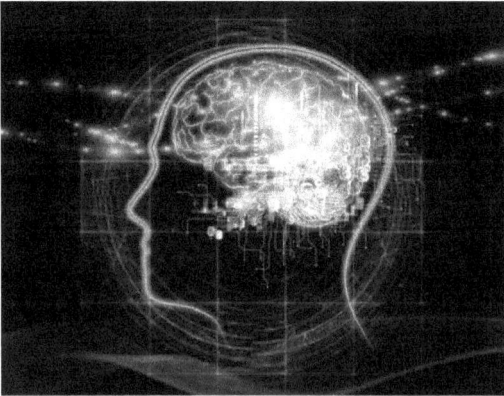

With the increased understanding of the extent to which Americans suffer from mental illness as well as enslavement issues and how expensive the total medical expenses are for this population we have reached an important tipping point when changes the way we think about healthcare. We recognize the importance of addressing the health requirements of those suffering from specific mental illnesses and responding to universal healthcare requirements all being the same. This is creating a series of opening doors for the conduct health network as well as a series of colossal challenges. mental health associations across in the U.S. are resolved to offer the ability and authority that aids the government offices, part associations and states, health plans and consumer groups to ensure that the major problems facing people suffering from mental health issues and addiction issues are properly addressed and integrated into changes to healthcare.

Expecting equality and mental healthcare reform implementation, the many nationwide and network mental health associations have been meeting, thinking and composing for over a whole year. Their work continues and the results are a factor in organizations that are promoting healthcare reform through government changes.

Mental Health Service Delivery

1. Mental Health/Substance Use Health Care Provider Capacity Building: The community mental health and substance abuse treatment associations, group practices, as well as individual clinicians need to improve their ability to offer high-performing, quantifiable Aversion and early mediation, recovery and wellbeing-oriented services and support.

2. Individual-Centered Healthcare Homes The future will see an increased interest in integrating mental health and substance use professionals into crucial contemplation practices as well as essential suppliers to the mental and drug use treatment organizations that are utilizing the latest and most effective practice clinical models , as well as robust connections between critical consideration and well-organized healthcare.

3. Friends Counselors and Consumer Operated Services We'll witness an expansion of the buyer managed administrations as well as a fusion of a look at those with mental illness and addiction abuse staff and the administration cluster and administration cluster, highlighting the main role these organizations play in aiding the healing and wellbeing of people suffering from mental illness and substance use issues.

4. Mental Health Clinic Guidelines: The speed of progress and dissemination of mental health drug use clinical guidelines and clinical tools will grow thanks to the newly created Patient-Centered Outcomes Research Institute as well as other implementation and research efforts. One aspect of this initiative involves helping patients suffering from mental illness find a mental health clinic nearby.

MENTAL Health SYSTEM management

5. Medicaid Expansion as well as Health Insurance Exchanges: States must consider

implementing significant changes to enhance the quality and efficiency of addiction and mental health administrations. They should revamp the Medicaid frameworks to develop and plan the structure of Health Insurance Exchanges. Supplier associations will likely join with new Medicaid structures, and also contract with and bill benefits through the Exchanges.

6. Business-sponsored Health Plans as well as Parity. Employers as well as benefits chiefs need to reclassify the way to use social health management to tackle presenters who do not appear and to build a more robust and more profitable workforce. Supplier associations must modify their contributions to deal with business-related issues and be in tune with their billing and contracting frameworks.

7. Responsible Care Organizations and Health Plan Redesign: Payments are empowered and will often control the evolution of new administrative structures

to support healthcare reform which includes Accountable Health Care Organizations as well as a health plan updates that will provide guidelines on how mental health care and drug use should be integrated to enhance quality and ensure the proper oversight of all health care consumption. Supplier associations should be a part of and become owners of ACOs which they create within their networks.

Mental Health Care INFRASTRUCTURE

8. Improvement in Quality Improvement for Mental Healthcare: The National Quality Forum and other organizations National Quality Forum will quicken the development of a national Quality Improvement Methodology that incorporates the execution of mental health and substance abuse estimations that are used to enhance the delivery of mental health and substance use services as well as tolerant health outcomes as well as the general health of the population

and monitor expenses. Associations of suppliers should create the base to operate within the system.

9. Healthcare Information Technology: Federal and state HIT initiatives should reflect the importance of mental health and substance abuse benefits, and include mental health as well as substance use suppliers as well as information needs in planning, financing and foundation development. Supplier associations must most likely establish electronic health records and patient libraries and integrate these frameworks with networked health systems, health data systems, and trade in data.

10. Healthcare Payment Reform Health and Payer plans should design and implement new installment components like capitation and cases which include esteem-based buying and esteem-based structure for protection techniques that are suitable for individuals with mental health and substance use issues. Providers

must modify their training, the board, charge frameworks as well as work forms to be compatible with the new system.

11. Employment Development: The major initiatives including the work of the new Workforce Advisory Committee will be required to develop an effective national workforce strategy to deal with the needs of people who suffer from mental illness and addiction use issues, including the expansion of advocates for friends. Supplier associations must be involved in these efforts and be ready to expand their workforce in order to meet unmet demand.

Mental Health What's It All About?

Mental Health is intertwined the ability to find harmony in managing the everyday challenges and taking advantage of the opportunities that life offers to improve. Mental power is vital to creating positive things in our lives. It is the instrument that allows us to move toward our hopes, dreams and hopes. Mental health is definitely more than just the absence of mental illness and is a part of many aspects of our lives including. Mental health concerns could be a sign of an increase in the risk of drinking alcohol smoking, smoking, and a an unsatisfactory eating regimen and physical health.

Stress, anxiety and depression can cause a lot of difficulty for seniors who face a lot of physical, energetic and financial changes that come with the transition to ageing. For instance, everyone knows that suffers from hypertension or diabetes or asthma is maladaptive when they stretch. They also have anxiety problems but do not be able to avoid psychiatric issues. Many who suffer from anxiety issues will try to avoid exposure to the things that cause anxiety.

When there is an anxiety problem the person will generally get nervous when confronted with a particular situation. For instance, for the person who nurtures mental health one could be thinking about and helping the mother who has post-natal severe depression or a young person who is struggling with the difficulties of a mental illness such as schizophrenia. or anxiety attacks that prevent them from working normally. Spiritual Power Symptoms for more youthful children. Stress and anxiety are the most prevalent health conditions.

Sadness is a normal condition and it's not just "life. Discouragement, which is the fastest-growing cause of long-distance incapacity across Canada is the most prevalent of these kinds of troubles that is characterized by bipolar issues (otherwise known as hyper sorrow) dysthymia, mania, and sometimes a feeling of problem. The research group has found that stress at work is linked to an overabundance risk of 50 percent of coronary disease, and there is a clear evidence that work with high an excessive amount of attention as well as low control exercise-related compensation irregularities are risk causes for physical and mental health problems (real anxiety, depression and issues with alcohol use).

With mental health concerns affecting the lives of one in four people within this region and is now one of the main reasons for not showing up at work, no one should remain naive regarding their mental health or that of their colleagues relatives, friends or friends. Mental Power Foundation Mental Power Foundation uses research and practical initiatives to assist people recover from, and prevent mental health problems. Mental health problems are complex physically, internally deeply, as well as socially.

Depression, sadness as well as panic attacks, are all common disorders, and would all be be treated effectively. Weight plays an important role in the health of your mind. Many people don't recognize that it's just as risky and as threatening as the other serious illnesses. People who are prone to this type of problem often create the conditions for further anxiety by the unchangeable expectations they have. Some experts suggest using positive self-talk and working to change the way that we perceive events can mitigate the mental and physical effects of managing stressful or difficult situations that happen in everyday life.

The signs of mental illness persist miserable, on edge or "void" behavior Agitation, anxiousness, frenziedness, or sadness, and grumpiness. Refrain from social and social situations or previously exuberant in exercise feeling of blame, ineffectiveness feelings of guilt, shame, or weight of despair and cynicism. Physical complaints that are difficult to acknowledge and are inaccessible to treatment. For example stomach related issues and cerebral pains, as well as heart palpitations and constant discomfort. Refusal to acknowledge the obvious difficulties Increasing inability to adjust to everyday challenges and exercises, or even minor problems Drinking alcohol or prescription medications and medication There are many types of mental disorders.

African Americans in this investigation did not show a clear connection between the symptoms that caused anxiety and the high-exertion adaptation methods, however Caribbean Blacks and white Americans noticed a growing sense of sadness that were correlated with increasing high-exercise changes, and the different beliefs and traits. Stress-related anxiety symptoms affect the satisfaction of a large number of people around the globe. The kind, force and duration of the symptoms differ from person to person however all mental illnesses can be treated.

The mental health of a person is the key to general physical health. Mental health is an Issue of human rights. In any event mental health goes beyond than just the absence of mental illness. Mental health issues aren't often able to be observed, however the signs can be observed.

Power of Mental Health Power of Mental Health

Health and mental wellness is something that we all require for ourselves regardless of whether or not we know it by name or not. There is no easy answer for this - mental wellbeing is like the obese stepchild that you took to the medical clinic of the state across the nation, and you only visited it once a year.

In reality, good mental health is a crucial component of overall health for those suffering from HIV. The Essential Care Mental Health is a different journal that is peer-reviewed and focuses that focuses on education, research development, and transmission of mental health as an essential aspect. In any event mental health is definitely more than the absence of mental illness.

It is the most effective way to deal with sorrows.

People are more likely to end a relationship in the event that their partner is believed to be suffering from severe depression or if they develop an incapacity physical. The two most reliable indicators for considering suicide were depression and abuse of substances.

Through convincing personal stories that are that are told on TV, video as well as the Internet and printed media, the campaign encourages people to see the effects of grief on their personal, professional and personal life. In addition, it will allow Cam-psyche to conduct the initiative to assist companies to manage stress, tension and sorrow in the workplace. What is the distinction between "normal" experiences of anxiety and those brought on by despair.

The subjects covered vary from a high level of confidence in puberty and signs of desperation to sources to diagnose mental health problems for children.

Chapter 9: The Oldies But Goldies:

They're Still Around For A Reason

Murphy's Law

We'll begin the discussion with a brief recap of the history behind Murphy's Law. Murphy's Law draws its origin or it is believed that it originated from a North Base air force base that was established in 1949. It is believed that it received its name by the well-known Edward. A Murphy. An engineer was working on an idea. This project was designed to reveal the feedback of the stress that a person can endure if the aircraft is destined to crash. In the course of his work that he was involved in, he came across an item of equipment known as a transducer that was repaired in a flawed manner. After a long and thoughtful discussion and apprehension, he made a vow that if he could find an opportunity for it to be fixed, and could be used incorrectly and he could find it. This is the reason that the contractor kept the list of laws and within it, he chose to include this specific phrase that is known as Murphy's Law. The significance of this particular law was a result of an old law that has been given shape and significance. Over the course of the subsequent decades, Murphy's Law gained fame and was quoted by a variety of people, not just to include the late Dr. John Paul Stapp. It was also the beginning of aerospace manufacturers taking the concept and starting to use it.

Murphy's Law draws its basis from a set of law known as the sod laws. Murphy, who had a personal identity was making sense of what the sods had previously been discussing. Murphy's Law draws its basis from Sod's law and, as such it tends to convey its respects to it since this is unfair to the sods. Sod's law Sods was one which has endured the test of period in the sense that its existence is more than that of a man. So, talking of Murphy's Law and failing to refer to Sod's law is just as a catastrophe. Sod's laws have gained significance by those in the Yorkshire families, and as such it is passed on through the majority of English jurisdictions. The name that was originally used for the law continues to diminish as the law's name is no longer well-known, and the information that people consider to be relevant is merely a matter of opinion. Murphy's Law encompasses nothing that is harmful or that undermines the laws of the Sods. It is believed that this kind of logic could not be discovered until later in the century of our time.

The most distinctive aspect of Murphy's Law is that it was created by a different person who was not Murphy. This person is known as Michael. Another belief that has been embraced to discredit the origins of Murphy's Law. To explain the law in a more straightforward manner it was said that if there were an incorrect way to do or doing something, then somebody will most likely perform it. That means that if there are a variety of options to get to an end point, then one of them would cause a disaster. If there's a possibility that something could happen, it will most likely happen.

In an attempt to give an understanding of the scientific quantity in Murphy's Law, we find that it makes sense of the possibilities of a certain outcome. This implies that there is a possibility of a variety of outcomes that result. When you look at the engineering behind it and you will see that no matter how efficient an item is and efficient, it will, in some way or other break down at an point. When you consider logic, you'll find that there are a variety of aspects of your life that can bring harmony. A lack of balance can lead to you live life in a stale manner, that can lead to monotony. There are many occasions in our lives that we do not feel happy to be able to remember. These are the times when caused us to feel the shame and the turmoil that we have caused to us. There's also a series of events that, upon connecting to, give us an underlying sense of belonging since those are the times where you were your most. The consequence from this is that one need to be prepared for these times of trouble because if there's an opportunity for something to go wrong taking place, it most certainly will happen.

A majority of those who are drawn in Murphy's Law are of the assumption that things aren't going to be as smooth In the majority of instances even if things do happen according to the way they would like, they're less grateful because they had an assumption that things wouldn't be straight. When the gas in thin air behaves the opposite direction, they begin to search for reasons for why they didn't be successful in what they were trying to accomplish. The importance of this law rests by our different abilities to achieve or fail in some thing. This law taps into that equilibrium. Most of the time it is evident that this law is operating through our subconscious.

The notion that we can't determine our fate is at the heart in this specific law. It is also known as the concept of fatalism. The basis of this is the idea that you do not have any control over what happen in your daily life. Consider, for instance, that the day we get up with the goal of getting to work. There is no way to predict the outcome of what is going to happen during the day. Murphy's Law is also supported by a law referred to as the law of Entropy. This is also known as the law that is natural to nature. It states that things will proceed in a way that appears appropriate. The majority of scholars have linked this law to the reason why individuals are in a stressful situation. Technology has given a foundation to this particular law since we are repeatedly reminded repeatedly that technology will not be able to function for forever.

Consequently it comes to a point that they'll fail.

Occam's Razor

This is a rule of thumb that can be said to mean that when there are two possible explanations for the same result. In this kind of reasoning it is the one that includes the smallest number of hypotheses is one that, is the most likely to perform. To define the concept, you will find how the less likely it is that you're to form more assumptions regarding a specific thing and the less likely you will be able to make a decision. The origins of this kind of principle are attributed to an individual named William Ockham. The man studied logic and created this particular kind of principle. If we refer to this concept in Latin the principle is known by the name of Lex Persimoniae. Others have also described it under the name of the law of conciseness. This law is of consequence that you have to be precise so that you don't generalize the majority of questions.

In a simpler way we could affirm that more resources cannot be used in a way than is essential.

In the world of life, there are numerous explanations for different results; this implies that it is possible that something could have taken place in several ways, but the one that is most accurate is the one that is close to the truth of the event. If there's an intricate explanation that is superior to a simpler one, then it is of crucial importance that the more complicated one is taken into account. This particular kind of concept seeks to provide explanations without focusing on the different entities accessible. This type of principle has the result of trying to provide an explanation of a specific issue in a way that is simple to understand. To clarify this specific type of concept, let's review one example.

Imagine that you awake early in the morning, and discover that you do not have a fence. There are two possible explanations for this specific phenomenon. One possibility is that the fence could be washed away by the rainstorms the night before or it could be a fallen aircraft which has destroyed the fence. Both of these scenarios are pertinent in the sense that they're bound to happen in one way or the other. The second, however must begin with a set of events to trigger its occurrence. The rarity of the second incident is the reason for the disqualification. The sequence of events which must happen before you discover the result of the second scenario is what supports the first one as possible to be wrong. The principle is based in the sense that if you consider the fact that there's an easy explanation that can be provided to the phenomena without a lot of jargon and if this is the best solution.

There are instances when the complex meaning that could be drawn from an item is usually the most accurate. It means that anyone who is conducting an evaluation has to be aware of several elements. It is possible to use this scenario that you are standing in a elevated area, and you hold in your hands the paper. The primary goal of this test is to determine the length of time it will require to hit the ground. Keep in mind that you need take into account the different factors which act as inhibitors that will result in an increment in time it is able to strike the floor. If you consider the air resistance, you are adding complexity to the matter. In order to make use of this principle it is possible to remove the influence of pressure in the air. In fact it is not the correct way to explain the amount of time the paper falls to the ground, as air resistance is an important factor in measuring the time it takes for the paper piece to fall. In order to provide an accurate time frame this explanation that follows is if it is accepted, could lead to a definitive assumption.

In the realm in medicine, this kind of theory has begun to expand. This has led to that the most straightforward explanation is one that involves thinking about a more intricate area. For instance, suppose there's one child who experiences breathing problems and wheezes. This child is much more likely to suffer from a common whooping cough, rather than linking this occurrence to a birth defect like Asthma. It is crucial that the signs be interpreted in their simplest way. This is so that you will not administer a substance that causes a huge impact. Physics employs this concept in the sense that it has the effect that for any fiction to have an effect it, there must be the use of a minimum amount of energy. In the realm of theology, this particular concept is considered to be pertinent because it is believed to facilitate the use of the Bible in the most straightforward way. It is a requirement for people to be devoid of many contradictions with the literal meaning of the bible, and prefer to take the bible as it is.

In terms of correctional facilities, you will find that those who have committed an offense are more likely to be to be sentenced to a minimum, except when the severity of the incident has gone beyond the limits of what is allowed. When it comes to criminal acts that are considered to be criminal, there are rules that address those who do not adhere to the co-existence agreement between the state and the populace. The provisions are usually made in a particular form which is specific to the punishment. Criminal justice systems, when imposing the punishments, must do so in a way that is of the lowest collator feasible. This is a change from the excessive punishments which were prevalent earlier.

Hanlon's Razor

As humans, there is a certain equilibrium that must be maintained. Due to this life is characterized by many events, ranging from bad to good. When positive things happen to us, we're overwhelmed to the point where we don't even notice the significance of these events. If something negative occurs we are forced to believe there was some plot behind the event occurring. For example, a person who does not submit your assignment on time because of a late rush. One of the thoughts in your head are that the person you are thinking of tends to go in your direction if you are failing. The answer at the heart of these theories is quite simple in the sense you'd like not to link your negative thinking with these accounts.

Hanlon's razor can be described as a kind of principle that could be explained in various ways. The most straightforward way you can explain this principle is that you shouldn't make the connection between any particular event to be based on maliciousness or malice to situations that have an origin in common sense. This kind of idea is essential in determining the possible causes of certain behaviors that are common to humans. Nature. This kind of concept has been affected by the razor of Occam. This principle has been applicable for a majority of people.

To summarize this rule, it is possible to conclude that you shouldn't refer to malice in the things that can be easy to explain by human behaviour. That means that negligence shouldn't be overlooked even when you think about the many negative outcomes. This kind of logic throughout our daily life, we are able to engage in deeper relationships with others. In this way, when someone wrongs us, we're in a position to allow them the space to be compassionate instead of shunning them immediately. A lot of people tend to be averse to others right after the first time. Based on this principle, you will find that you're in a position of giving people a second chance because you think that everyone is a human being and will make mistakes in one way or the other.

In our daily adventures, we discover that we tend to be in contact with other people. through this communication we are forced to make decisions that affect the way we live our lives. This is why we experience the challenges of life. You'll find yourself in a situation in which things aren't functioning as they should and you're making mistakes over and over time. If this happens, we do not like to take the blame on ourselves, but instead to blame another person. It is usually the person right next to us. It is due to the idea that they could have a motive to harm us. When it comes to transferring responsibility to other people, they are quick to judge others and commit. When we are near someone else who is committing a mistake and we are prone to overlook the many instances that we've messed up. The problem in human beings is that we are prone to ignore the numerous instances that we've done wrong to someone else , and instead focus on the offenses other people have caused us.

If you believe that there was a malicious intention behind the event, you discover that you are likely to exacerbate the situation. This is due to the fact that no one has control over what other people wanted to accomplish. Many people who are smart in different areas of life have been discovered to be likely to make numerous errors. It is because mistakes are a common thing that is not caused by the character of an individual, but rather the normal process of life. When we are on edge of being overwhelmed by emotions, it's important to consider the reality that we are likely to act in this way whenever we feel angry. Once we come to recognize this that we're better positioned to respond positively to these circumstances. Situations that cause us to become upset and angry are of the times those which are the most important to us.

The best method of dealing with people who cause us anxiety and stress is to impart a simple lesson to them. This will show them that you're more important than they are And by doing this you can make sure that the same issue does not occur again. Media has been one of the parties that play a significant part in this particular aspect. It is evident that the media is a source of incidents that are characterized as a rage from one who was ignorant or incompetent. As technology advances that are taking place in media we are able to discover those cases that were accompanied by the ill-gotten gains of malice. Anything that contains the appearance of the presence of malice has appeared to be found.

In the case of relationships, it is evident that this specific principle is applied in a manner that's essential. The main issue that stems in all relationships is that you feel the other person has become toxic. In this manner you'll discover that the other person is at the root of your issues. Once you've established that then you can begin to figure out ways you can break up with the relationship as it is harmful to you. A lot of individuals who've been involved in relationships say that letting the inside feeling of malice build up can cause the relationship to eventually breaking down. This kind of scenario is observed in those who are experiencing a difficulty. The majority of people is drawn to the notion that they cannot understand the meaning of what they are saying. This kind of law will mean that it is not beneficial to keep you from being a victim.

Chapter 10: Mental Models For More Positive Thinking

Positive thinking may seem like an insignificant phrase that's employed in self-help books or talk shows, but the truth is that it's extremely effective. The positive effects of a conscious attitude can affect your physical health, since multiple studies have shown that there's the connection between positive thoughts and the prevention of illnesses. On the other end from the other side, negative thoughts and stress can affect your physical and mental health even impacting the immune system.

The reason why people are skeptical of positive thoughts is because on the surface , it seems like denial of reality. But, this isn't what positive thinking is actually about. The focus is on managing your expectations, recognizing negativity, and getting free of destructive thought patterns. In this section, we'll discuss mental models that will help boost your positive outlook.

#1. The Pratfall Effect

In 1966, a social psychology Elliot Aronson conducted an experiment. He believed that those who are thought to be "superior" in the sense that they are more popular in the event of small errors or "pratfalls." For his study the researcher recorded a variety of people responding to questions, and watched other participants in the study. One person could answer 92 percent correct and then gave a short biographical sketch of himself that included: he was an honors student at high school and a track runner and also an editor of the yearbook. Then, at the end of the tape, the listeners were shocked to hear an individual who was considered to be the "superior" person said, "I spilled coffee on my new dress." Following the tape was played the test participants gave their thoughts. The person who was thought to be "superior" gained more respect after spilling his coffee.

Pratfall Effect Pratfall Effect can be very helpful if you struggle with the pressure to achieve perfection. It doesn't matter if it's at workplace or within your friends, you are always striving to be the most perfect. As you get more well-known and successful and respected, the thought of falling down can be a bit scary. You may begin to feel as if you're a fraud, and worry that you'll commit a mistake and the world will see that you're not the best. Be aware of your Pratfall Effect in mind and keep in mind that it's OK for you to fail. Actually, it makes you more relatable to others and people will begin to respect and admiring you more. The way you frame failures and mistakes by imagining them in this manner will improve your overall optimism and outlook.

What if you don't believe that you are superior in any way? Aren't your mistakes likely to make you undesirable? Although it is true that Pratfall Effect study defined "superior" in a very particular way, the truth is that, even though you might not consider yourself to be any sort of a celebrity but there are those within your circle who think of you as such. This may not be the case all the time in you life but, they could think of you as the perfect parent, the ideal sister, the perfect employee and the list goes on. Although you are aware that your life is not perfect, some people might think you are "having all the things." Being open about your flaws and flaws with those who you trust brings you closer to one another.

#2. Entropy

If you are constantly disinterested in your life If you are struggling to stay motivated, the mental model of entropy can assist you in regaining your motivation. The concept "entropy" is actually derived out of the second thermodynamic law which says that everything tends to decrease over time, shifting from order to chaos.

Entropy can be found in every aspect that is in our universe which includes humans. Our bodies age and begin to break down. While this may sound sad but it could be an incentive to you to rise and take action. It is possible to delay the process of entropy if you do something and every action aids.

What can this model do to be applied to positive thinking? It frames every choice you make as a struggle against decay and chaos. Everything you do is important. All of it helps to push away from the normal degeneration of the world. This is why the Entropy model isn't suitable for anyone as it has negative effects, creating the illusion that nothing is worth doing since every thing has the possibility of expiring. If, however, you're already well aware that nothing is eternal and you are aware that you control over entropy could help to get you back on track and taking action.

Entropy is also a tool to identify aspects of your life that aren't effective or sustainable, since it is believed that whenever you invest your energy into something, it's going to bring order to it. If something is that you're living (like your job or relationship) that doesn't consistently bring order or meaning back that's not worth investing in.

#3. The Spotlight Effect

Spotlight Effect Spotlight Effect is a mental model that nearly everyone has in their minds, but it's not true. According to this theory that there's always a spotlight around you all the time and everyone has a view of every aspect of you, particularly the flaws and unnatural actions you take. However, the reality is that most people are focused on their own lives: everyone is a spotlight for themselves. When you realize that you are experiencing the Spotlight Effect in your own mind and accept that nobody actually notices or is interested in about what you're doing, you can take away some of the anxiety.

Let's say you're suffering from anxiety about social situations and you're attending a party. You're at the end of the aisle and are worried that everyone is staring at you in a sideways manner, and judging your outfit. The idea of having to make these judgments can be overwhelming and you're scared to even speak since you're afraid of saying something stupid. If this happens, be aware of your Spotlight Effect. The people aren't focused on you in any way. They're probably thinking of themselves. Some of them might share the same fears as that you have. The room is filled with individuals who are being filmed in their minds. should someone later inquire about what someone else had been wearing that day, the likely won't have any memory.

The realization that nobody is all the time looking at you is a liberating feeling. There is no need to think constantly about what others are thinking and instead, you are able to live your life. If you slip up or do something that you think is foolish, the chances are that no one else will pay attention. Your thought process will be more clear if you're not overwhelmed by anxiety and fears regarding the opinion of other people.

#4. The Pygmalion Effect

The legend of Pygmalion is an account of the life story of a statue (named Pygmalion) who carves an exquisite sculpture of a woman. It's so realistic that he is in love with it. He begins treating the statue as real people, talking to her and acting like she's his wife. The gods are impressed by his love for the statue and the statue is transformed into an actual woman. It is believed that the Pygmalion Mental model takes its name from this tale and states that having expectations are the key to successes. Pygmalion believed that his statue was real and had extremely high expectations and it ended being what he imagined.

In the latter half of the 1960's In the 1960's, the researchers Jacobsen as well as Rosenthal conducted research and found that teacher expectations can influence the performance of students. They discovered that expectations high resulted in positive effects on students while lower expectations caused the opposite. They dubbed their findings the Pygmalion Effect. This is applicable to the expectations you place on yourself. Do you think of yourself as an able person? Do you think of yourself as someone who's that is bound to fail? It's a self-fulfilling prediction both ways. If you are confident that you will be successful, you're significantly more likely to succeed in reaching your objectives (or at least come close) as opposed to if you have negative thoughts about your potential.

The Pygmalion Effect inspires individuals to push themselves further and to raise their standards. It's an excellent example of the good qualities which can result from taking on the challenge. This mental model demonstrates that both negative and positive thinking can have a direct impact on the outcome. What kind of thinking would you like to influence your life?

#5. The Looking-Glass Self

Based on the Looking-Glass self idea, developed through Charles Horton Cooley way back in 1902, our perception of self-worth isn't derived from within us, it's derived through our interactions with people and what we think that they have about us. The mental model suggests that those around us are reflections or looking glasses through which we perceive our personal identity. We alter our actions based on what we imagine we're seeing in order to feel loved and accepted. If we think someone else is disapproving of us or disapproving of our actions Our self-esteem and self-esteem can be shaken.

What is the way that the Looking-Glass self-model work? Let's suppose you're visiting your parents. You're talking about a film you watched recently. As you're discussing the story, you observe people looking sad and frowning. They don't seem to like the film, and you conclude that if you liked the film, your parents aren't going to like it also. Your self-esteem is shattered and your negative self-talk takes over. In the next moment, you're talking to someone else who has also seen the film and was really impressed with it, so you inform them that you enjoyed it too. In both instances you're showing various versions of yourself to get accepted.

Who are we , other than reflections of what other people think? Our sense of self-identity and the way in which we define it will be influenced through the views of other people It is likely that you'll lose your personal identity within the crowd of people who are your looking-glass self to navigate through your social life. This could lead to low self-esteem, depression anxiety and other mental health problems. Be aware of how much you rely on others to maintain your self-worth is vital in improving your mental wellbeing and avoiding negative thinking. Accept you won't always appreciate or appreciate you, and that's ok. Find your own inner mirror and cultivate the connections that help you to have an optimistic view of yourself. You'll notice a significant increase in self-esteem.

#6. Maslow's Hierarchy of Needs

in 1943 Abraham Maslow proposed that every human being has an orderly hierarchy of requirements. To be a fully developed, content person, this hierarchy should be present throughout the course of one's life. Maslow created the hierarchy in an encapsulated pyramid with five levels. From the bottom upwards the basic needs are:

Physical needs such as water, food and shelter. etc.

Security needs such as physical and mental security

Conclusion

You've done it. You've made the first step to becoming more focused, self-controlled and successful person thanks to your newfound understanding of mental models. I wish that your journey doesn't end here. While this book offered an extensive overview of many mental models there are many different models to choose from.

There may be an idea that resonates with you, but was not discussed by these sections. You owe it to yourself and the future of your career to identify the mental models that perform best for you.

Thank you for taking the time to read this book up to the very close. I hope you found it an interesting read that was can provide you with additional tools to help you achieve your goals, however they might be.

Do you recall the moment you started to read this book and I suggested at the end in the intro to consider your objectives and the book could accomplish for them? Consider them today. Have they been modified or changed? Are you adding to your list of goals you'd like to do? Make use of the momentum acquired by studying psychological models and make improvements in your lifestyle to reach your goals. Your routines and habits must reflect who you wish to be and the results you'd like to achieve. Are they? What do you need to do, utilizing the information we've shared in this book, to modify your daily routine to reflect the person you'd like to be in the coming year?

One of the tools for mental models, which is discussed in this book in a brief manner, but not at length it is journaling. Making a notepad as well as making it your goal to fill it up will assist to build every mental model regardless of what you are trying to achieve. For a continuation of the journey that you began by reading this book, head out and get your notebook. What you'll find when you record your thoughts on mental models:

Note down the things you'd like to achieve can make your plans and goals more than a mere thought. Writing down your dreams on paper, you're making a commitment for yourself to make it happen. the job done.

If you have trouble setting goals, journaling with prompts can help determine what you want to accomplish and the reasons. Don't let the term 'goal cause you to be paralyzed. A goal is simply an indicator of miles in the way to where you'd like to get to. Writing about your final goal will help you determine what the mile markers could appear like.

* Writing helps to identify passions that you didn't even know existed before. Writing can often feel like meditation. It's a chance to completely be present in your thoughts. So, ideas come out of your mind naturally when you're focused on you along with your future.

When you journal, you'll discover that certain mental models, such as those of the Eisenhower Matrix, are just more easily seen on paper. It's difficult to keep the track of tasks and lists when they're all scattered in your head.

Journaling can help you keep an eye on your gratitude routine. It's fascinating to look back over a long time and find out the things you were grateful for at the time and also what you've lost track of, but which you can revive your energy in the present.

182

* Certain ways of writing such as journaling with the Bullet Journal, can also aid in keeping you organized and be a element of your discipline program. Journaling in a structured manner can help you to keep track of your routines and schedule. It can also give you an additional boost to enthusiasm by providing you with a container to mark off each task completed.

Mental models are amazing tools, but they're only that: tools. There is no self-help program or psychological trick will lead you to success. They are available for you to gather and perhaps utilize however, just as Maya Angelou famously said, it's impossible to succeed without you. If you truly want to see your goals come true before you the only person most likely to achieve that is you.

You're the only person who can bring your dreams to reality. You're the only person who's enthusiastic enough and eager to see your future become as stunning as you've thought it would be. The only thing that can guarantee to perform as well as your own determination and passion for the goals you have set. That's it. The conclusion of the line. Go get 'em, tiger.

www.ingramcontent.com/pod-product-compliance
Lightning Source LLC
Chambersburg PA
CBHW060330030426
42336CB00011B/1278